Spotlight on Making Music with Special Learners

Spotlight on Making Music with Special Learners

Selected Articles from State MEA Journals

Published in partnership with
MENC: The National Association for Music Education
Frances S. Ponick, Executive Editor

Rowman & Littlefield Education
Lanham • New York • Toronto • Plymouth, UK

Published in partnership with
MENC: The National Association for Music Education

Published in the United States of America
by Rowman & Littlefield Education
A Division of Rowman & Littlefield Publishers, Inc.
A wholly owned subsidiary of The Rowman & Littlefield Publishing Group, Inc.
4501 Forbes Boulevard, Suite 200, Lanham, Maryland 20706
www.rowmaneducation.com

Estover Road
Plymouth PL6 7PY
United Kingdom

First Rowman & Littlefield Education edition 2007

British Library Cataloguing in Publication Information Available

Library of Congress Control Number: 2006929644

ISBN-13: 978-1-56545-167-4
ISBN-10: 1-56545-167-8

∞™ The paper used in this publication meets the minimum requirements of
American National Standard for Information Sciences—Permanence of
Paper for Printed Library Materials, ANSI/NISO Z39.48-1992.
Manufactured in the United States of America.

Contents

The *Spotlight* series comprises articles that have appeared in magazines of MENC affiliates over the past several years. The purpose of the series is to broaden the audience for the valuable work that is being done by music educators across the country. Were it not for the dedication of the state editors and article authors, this series would not be possible. MENC would like to thank these individuals for their contributions and to encourage others to share their expertise through MEA and MENC publications.

Introduction

> The curriculum for all pupils in the Primary or Advanced Class, whether hearing or deaf, embraces the English elementary branches, as follows: ... Music: Vocal, including imitative accurate singing, kindergarten songs and games, etc., being led by adult or piano.[1]
>
> —*Program description of the Kindergarten and Primary School for Hearing and Deaf Children, Washington DC, founded in 1883 by Alexander Graham Bell*

Including music in the curriculum for special learners is not a new idea. The quote above is one of the first textual references to actual music teaching for students who have hearing impairments.[2] However, the role of music in special education has largely been ignored until recently. Even in his *History of Public School Music in the United States*,[3] published in 1929, Edward Bailey Birge makes no mention of special learners.

Thanks to the growing acceptance of all kinds of learners and the legislation passed since 1975, special learners are increasingly being included in music classes. Some of these classes are only for special learners, others practice inclusion—having students with disabilities participate in regular classes.

These trends have led music teachers to adjust their curriculums to teach all these different kinds of learners, cope with children having various disabilities, and still support their students who are not special learners. And, they have often had to do this without additional training, specific information about their students, or the assistance available to the classroom teacher.

The articles in *Spotlight on Making Music with Special Learners* will help you with special learners whether you teach chorus, band, orchestra, or general music. One thread that runs consistently through the articles is how all children learn in different ways and that the strategies typically used to teach special learners will help all the students in your class. There are ideas for getting the assistance you need, strategies for curriculum adaptation, advice on how to enlist the help of your administration, and stories to encourage you.

Though some teachers struggle with the special learners in their classes, and others have no difficulty teaching them, in the end, no matter what challenges students face, they make you realize that all children are just that, children.

Notes

1. Edward Allen Fay, ed., *History of American Schools for the Deaf 1817–1893* (Washington DC: *The Volta Review*, 1893), vol. 3, p. 6.

2. Alan L. Solomon, "Music in Special Education before 1930: Hearing and Speech Development, *Journal of Research in Music Education* 28 (Winter 1980): 236–42.

3. Edward Bailey Birge, *History of Public School Music in the United States* (Reston, VA: MENC, 1929).

Music Educators: Hidden Allies for Poor Readers

Elaine Bernstorf

Who is the most likely consultant for a child who experiences reading or writing problems? The classroom teacher, reading specialist, or special education teacher, right? Music teachers are not usually considered "reading" teachers, although they may frequently be defined as the teachers of "specials." In educational settings, the term "specials" is often used to refer to music, art, dance/movement, drama, P. E., or library. The terms "special education" or reading specialist are used to refer to "special" educational strategies that may be "less conventional or less traditional" than those strategies typically used for teaching large groups of children to listen, think, speak, read, write, or do math. Most often those "less conventional" strategies involve the breaking down of tasks into smaller, sequential steps through a process called "task analysis." In the process of "task analysis," a teacher separates each skill to be learned into subunits which include specific actions, concepts, vocabulary, and sequences. Prerequisite skills are defined which need to be taught before the desired task can be introduced. When the desired skill is then to be taught, the teacher will have observed others do the task, noted the steps in the tasks, tried the steps to be sure of the specificity and sequence, and finally mastered the skill in order to teach the child.

So, what does the process of "task analysis" and "reading" have to do with music education? Music education introduces students to a discipline which explores the wonders of sound and symbol in ways that compliment, yet are quite different than those we traditionally think of as "reading." The purpose of this short article is to encourage music educators to embrace their role as allies to other teachers for students who may be lost in the traditional world of sounds and symbols we know as "Reading."

We speak of "reading" literature, "reading" music, "reading" another's thoughts, "reading" the situation. Music teachers do all of this and more. They introduce students to an exciting world where small circles with little sticks on the side ride on top of the roads of five long lines which travel from left to right across the wide expanse of white known as a page of music. However, music teachers also introduce students to the exciting world where these small circles and well traveled roads intersect with beautiful sounds which can be made by a variety of sound sources. One of the sound sources is the voice. When vocal sound is used, there is a lovely choice. The vocal sound may have only one level of meaning, the movement of the music with its pitches, durations, intensities, and color quality. However, the vocal sound may also convey specific language, a second layer of meaning. The language may move in synchrony with the music, syllable by syllable, word by word, phrase by phrase, section by section. Or, the language may be blended into the musical offering to the point that the listener and singer must carefully unravel the artistic tapestry that is created in order to look at the individual threads that are "music" and that are "language." In fact, many would argue that music *is* language, a universal language.

The purpose of this article is not to focus on the aesthetic components of music and language which are so valuable for students, but rather to look at some of the "processes" used when students experience music and language through specific study of the disciplines or "intelligences" as described by Howard Gardner (1986). When Gardner spoke of his definition of intelligences, he referred to common characteristics that he said helped "define" an intelligence. Among those characteristics is the use of a symbol system or agreed upon "codes" for those who work within that area of intelligence. Such is true for the linguistic intelligence, where alphabets are used to convey information, and for music, where several code systems exist simultaneously. In music, the codes depict the frequency (pitch), intensity (dynamics), time/duration (meter, rhythm, tempo), and manner (articulation) of individual sounds and groups of sounds. When a specific word text is added, the code system is even more detailed. As complex as the tasks of reading language and reading music may be, in music we have some advantages. In music classes, teachers frequently break apart the different codes and manipulate the specific aspects of the sound which is associated with those codes. In the study of music, students separate sections of music and phrases into specific patterns and even separate pitches. These tasks allow students to explore small aspects of sound and symbol. In language reading, teachers work with students to separate the sounds of words into individual phonemes. In such a situation "cat" actually becomes the sounds /k/ /æ/ /t/ (International Phonetic Alphabet). But for many students, these tasks are extremely difficult. As music educators, we may be able to help students associate sounds and symbols by manipulating sounds in more than one way. We have the option of manipulating sound in ways that do not carry linguistic associations. The same parameters of pitch, dynamics, duration, and articulation which make sounds musical can transcend linguistics. Music can exist with or without words. This quality makes learning to read music truly "special."

Common Aspects of Reading Language and Reading Music

It may be that one of the aspects we should consider as music educators is the similarity between oral language reading and music reading as the ability to "process a sequential presentation of visual code in order to assign meaning through sound." The "matching" of sound to symbol is a critical component of successful reading. We as music educators have a tremendous opportunity to assist students in ways that may not be available in regular "language" reading instruction. Consider some of the tasks we use to assist students in music reading. The following paragraphs discuss a few examples of specific tasks used in reading language and music. This discussion is not inclusive nor tied to a specific music or reading method. The tasks are simply common tasks associated with preliteracy and early literacy activities in the areas of music and language. It should be noted that there are many areas of overlap between the two disciplines when "reading" is considered. However, there are some areas where music educators have additional tasks which may assist students in associating sounds with visual graphics (icons) and symbols. It is these tasks which may ultimately allow music educators to become hidden allies to students who experience reading problems.

Early Preliteracy Skills

General visual orientation in reading. Both music and language reading require a general orientation to visual representations of sound. Early reading experiences in both areas include pointing to pictures of items which are heard. Most children have experiences where they point to pictures of animals, musical instruments, vehicles, etc. when they hear the sounds produced by those sources. Children frequently point out visual examples of musical notation when they hear music, or they may produce musical "la la la" sounds when they see musical notation. This orientation to musical and language symbols is an important preliteracy skill. Music educators have an advantage, however, in that they may help children "read" musical sound in a more generic way even before children can understand specific musical symbols. Teachers who use visual icons of long and short lines to show musical duration (e.g., __ __ ____ for short–short–long) or who use directional lines to show the pitch movement of music (e.g., ↑ or ↓) have an additional type of subtask which may assist children who may have potential reading problems with more "general" orientations to sound. In language reading, there is some use of "rebus" visuals (these are pictures that stand for words). However, the use of rebus cues is almost exclusively for nouns. Rarely do rebus visuals give the type of specific sound-graphic associations that are found in musical icons.

Spatial orientation/association in reading. Parents are always excited when their small children make the association between letters and words. They watch small fingers begin to separate strings of rapid scribbles into individual squiggles, knowing that the child is beginning to "write." Parents beam when a child brings a smattering of those squiggles and says, "I made you a card," or "I wrote you a letter." Parents also notice when children begin to reorient books or papers so that the writing is right-side up.

Beginning Reading Skills

Segmentation/syllablization in reading. Children who are exposed to music notation may begin to associate the spatial orientation of the notation with the individual sounds of music. Many early childhood music programs allow children to use various objects as manipulatives to associate sounds with symbols. Magnetic circles placed on a painted staff can show melodic direction. Parents and teachers who point to the separate syllables and the musical notes associated with those syllables in hymnals and other printed vocal music provide children with additional experiences with sound segmentation. In this case, vocal music may provide the best opportunities for beginning readers of both music and language.

Auditory-visual discrimination. Simple music where each syllable directly matches a musical pitch will provide the most direct learning transfers. Music with melismatic (multiple pitches for a single syllable) passages may need additional explanation. Such examples require students to synthesize isolated pitches into a musical whole word. This requires **auditory-visual blending.** Music that is printed with multiple verses under the musical pitches can be confusing for students when the number of syllables does not match the number of musical notes printed above those syllables. With careful attention to these details and the use of visual icons, additional visual examples on overhead transparencies, blackboards, or separately printed examples, teachers can use such confusing situations to actually assist students in reading tasks. In these situations, teachers assist the students with **auditory and visual figure ground.** The fact that the same musical structure is repeated as each verse is sung except for those "special" differences pointed out by the teacher, gives the students an auditory template with which to compare their visual reading symbols. Learning becomes a mental game of finding the specific differences in the same context. The auditory cues provided by the musical line allow those differences to almost jump off the page and students learn to discriminate between what they see and what they hear. When students become adept at music-language reading they will actually predict what should come next. Such predictions are heard when students begin to recognize repeated patterns or sing the appropriate pitch within the tonal context when sight-reading. For example, children will begin to end on the tonic even when they are singing made-up songs (Wedel, 1993). Such predictions are examples of auditory and visual closure which are additional important skills in reading.

Auditory-visual memory and sequential memory. Language reading has some examples of this type of similar context with highlighted differences in rhyming books. Dr. Seuss books provide many good examples of a predictable context with highlighted novelty differences. Consider the book *One Fish, Two Fish, Red Fish, Blue Fish* (Seuss, 1981). For several pages, only the first word changes (One fish, two fish, red fish, blue fish. Black fish, blue fish, old fish, new fish). Later, only the last word changes (This one has a little star. This one has a little car.) And finally a whole new sentence (Say, what a lot of fish there are.). But then the pattern repeats with a slight variation (Some are old and some are new. Some are bold and some are blue. Some are mad and some are sad. And some are very, very bad.) And another contrast (Why are they sad and glad and bad? I do not know, go ask your Dad!). Did Dr. Seuss realize he was using such a wonderful example of AB form with small variations within the A section? The "musical feel" of many Dr. Seuss books encourages a "sing-song" approach to the reading. As a result, children respond, remember, and read.

Summary

The specific tasks and associated skills described in this article reflect the observations of a music educator who is also a speech pathologist. Reading tasks appear in a variety of activities associated with any child's educational experiences. Educators with a variety of backgrounds in music, reading, early childhood education, and language development will each have additional insights with which to consider these observations. As music educators, our awareness of the types of skills needed to read music and our awareness of similarities to language reading may assist us in providing experiences appropriate for all students and especially beneficial to students who have difficulty in reading. The very reading activities that we provide also provide auditory-visual associations that help bridge the gap for poor readers. Additional time in silent reading may not be the answer for some students. Additional time in active music reading with an educator who understands specific qualities of sound and symbol may be one answer that needs additional exploration.

References

Gardner, H. (1986). *Frames of mind.* New York: Basic Books.

Hansen, D., & Bernstorf, E. (2002). Linking music learning to reading instruction. *Music Educators Journal*, 17, pp. 17–12, 52.

Nicolosi, L., Harryman, E. & Kresheck, J. (1989). *Terminology of communication disorders: Speech-language-hearing.* Baltimore, MD: Williams and Wilkins.

Seuss, Dr. [Theodor Seuss Geisel] (1981). *One fish, two fish, red fish, blue fish.* New York: Random House.

Wedel, S. (1993). Spontaneous song: Comparison of normal and language-delayed kindergarteners. Master's thesis. Wichita State University.

This article first appeared in the 2003 Convention issue of the Kansas Music Review. *Reprinted by permission.*

Breaking Ground: Role Models for All Your Students

Ruth V. Brittin

Did you ever have a role model? Someone who encouraged you to practice, persevere, take a risk, or try something new? Maybe it was a professional musician—someone you had never met, but had read about or heard in concert or on a recording. Perhaps it was a family member or even a slightly older student who inspired you to push ahead. Maybe a music teacher gave you an extra measure of attention or showed certain qualities you hoped to emulate.

We probably have all benefitted from some musical role models and tried to be good examples for our students. Certainly the values we model have an impact. However, we also know that our student populations are changing, and with this changing world, we may need to expand our inspirational resources—both for our students and for ourselves!

The American population is changing in its racial composition, with an increased emphasis on multiculturalism. We also see an increase in the inclusion of students with varying abilities and skills. The Americans with Disabilities Act of 1991, for example, built on over two decades of mainstreaming. Teachers see students from more varied backgrounds and with more diversity in interests, skills, and abilities than ever before. As we encounter students with "new" characteristics, we may wonder whether these children can succeed on particular instruments, in certain ensembles, or with selected musical genres. It helps to look at examples where others have succeeded in unusual situations.

We see from a number of studies over the years (Abeles & Porter, 1978; Fortney, Boyle, & DeCarbo, 1993; Zervoudakes & Tanur, 1994) that gender is an issue that can influence instrument selection. Many articles, books, and dissertations have been written exploring the effect of society on a girl's potential success on a "boy's instrument." Certainly the women succeeding at the highest levels of performance on wind and percussion instruments have provided a strong role model for younger players.

Gender clearly is not the only societal issue influencing young people's musical decisions. Concerning ethnic background, Hamaan and Walker (1993) found that African American students were more likely to consider a career in music if they had worked with an African American music teacher. Thus students may be more successful if they perceive certain commonalities between themselves and the teacher.

Certainly a long-term approach is to establish a more diverse teacher population. However, teachers will always be faced with teaching students from different backgrounds, regardless of who is in the majority or minority at a particular school. Since role models do appear to be so important, we should be ready to identify inspirational musicians with whom the student shares commonalities. These commonalities might include race, cultural identity, gender, ability level, or socioeconomic status, but may also hinge on other values as well.

How does one expose students to a wider range of role models, when time seems so short? Who are some of the musicians that students might not encounter through the popular media, but who would serve as positive musical role models? The instrumentalists mentioned here represent only a few of the "success stories" to which a music teacher might point.

Evelyn Glennie is a professional percussionist with a highly acclaimed solo career. Born in Scotland, Glennie began piano at age eight, clarinet two years later, and then percussion at age 12, despite the fact that she had become profoundly deaf after she began losing her hearing at age six. Glennie studied percussion at the Royal Academy of Music in London, where she won numerous awards for percussion, tympani, orchestral playing, and all-around performance and academic accomplishment. Since then, Glennie has had many recital pieces written for her, has performed internationally with celebrated symphony orchestras, has recorded extensively, and has been the subject of several documentaries. She published her autobiography, entitled *Good Vibrations*, in 1990 at the age of 24.

Music teachers might be interested in Glennie's recollections of her early music studies (Vogel, 1989). Upon entering secondary school and expressing an interest in percussion, Glennie was required to take an aural musical test. She had not admitted to the music teachers that she was deaf and only scored a few points out of the exam's possible 100. Although the teachers initially did not want to accept her, she began to work with the percussion teacher, Ron Forbes. She describes her first attempts at tympani tuning as follows.

> I just could not do it! ... One day he had me stand outside the percussion room and put my hands flat on the wall. He then tuned the two timpani to a wide interval and asked me which drum he was

> playing on, the higher or the lower. Then he asked, "How do you know? Where are your feeling that?" I could feel the vibrations in my hands and lower parts of my legs, so I got the pitch that way. Gradually the interval became closer and closer, and I could not only tell which drum was being played, but what the interval was. (pp. 46–47)

Glennie herself works with numerous organizations for the deaf; however, she would rather be known as a role model for all young musicians, rather than only for young deaf musicians (Walsh, 1994). This brings to light an important point. Role models are multifaceted in their attributes, and they may inspire students for a variety of reasons.

Other musical role models might include performers such as Rafael Mendez. Rafael was raised in Mexico, served as Pancho Villa's cornetist while still a boy, immigrated to the United States, and became one of history's greatest trumpet players, inspiring young musicians across the world (Hickman, 1994). In addition to setting an extremely high performance standard, he contributed to the field's literature. He recorded the standards of the trumpet literature, but also diversified the repertoire by arranging and recording many Mexican folk songs. Hickman's biography lists these pieces of literature, as well as a very thorough discography, with information on where material may be obtained.

Another inspirational trumpet performer is Carole Dawn Reinhart, an American who became the first woman to study trumpet at the Vienna Academy of Music, to receive a diploma from the academy on a brass instrument, and to be appointed to the brass, woodwind, and percussion faculty there. In her biography, she comments on her first memories of developing a professional goal.

> The first time I considered becoming a professional musician was during an orientation class in seventh grade. We were given the assignment to write a term paper about a chosen career. Approximately ten girls raised their hands to become teachers, about five for nursing and the others, to become secretaries. For some reason, I wanted to choose something that no one else in the class would write about, so I selected professional trumpeter. I was fascinated by the planning of my paper, and most especially the cover (my artistic background!). My idol, Rafael Mendez, had a silhouette of a trumpeter on his arrangements. I copied this silhouette. ... It made a stunning impression. (Ostleitner and Simek, 1994, pp. 98–99)

She also realized that professional musicians of the era (the early 1950s) were earning three to four times the amount that secretaries earned, and that inspired her to take the risks of what seemed to many a questionable career choice.

Some musicians have battled physical traumas to pursue their musical careers. For example, Itzhak Perlman's bout with polio did not dampen his enthusiasm for studying violin; indeed, the instrument provided an outlet in which he could rise above the limitations associated with such a disability. The pianist Leon Fleisher (a San Francisco native) also refused to succumb to the ravages of repetitive stress syndrome on his right hand. He continued to teach at prestigious conservatories, conduct, and administer music festivals such as Tanglewood. He performed—and continued to expand—the piano literature for left hand alone. In 1995, Fleisher again began performing select two-hand literature and has performed in recent years with the San Francisco Symphony.

Other musicians have explored music in unconventional ways, such as Wynton Marsalis, who is admired for both his jazz and classical work. Willie Ruff, a respected jazz French horn player, is another positive example. As part of the Mitchel-Ruff Duo, he performs, records, and lectures on jazz internationally. He has taught on the faculty at the Yale School of Music for 30 years and is founding director of the Duke Ellington Fellowship Program there. Ruff, an African American who grew up in rural Alabama in the 1930s, reveals many of the inspirations, challenges, and victories of aspiring musicians in his 1992 autobiography, *A Call to Assembly*. In it, we glimpse not only his associations with performers and composers such as Duke Ellington and Billy Strayhorn, but we also gain insight into a person who has broken stereotypes for decades.

These musicians are not only inspirational, but are accessible to students through the media. All are easily searchable on the Internet. All have been recorded and are the subjects of biographies, published interviews, and video. Music teachers, however, may need to look for strategies to expose young people to such figures, rather than hoping that students will simply stumble across the information. To do so, consider structuring a reason for students to search out this information. For example, suggest to students they use such role models for English papers, social studies reports, or history projects. On your bulletin board post a list of suggested artists which students can access when they need to develop a topic for another class. Ask students to post Web site information when they find really helpful Web sites on their own.

Other ideas include developing your own library of CDs and videotapes featuring inspirational musicians. Have these on hand for days when the schedule changes or you have a substitute teacher. Allow students to review them for extra credit. Include materials that challenge stereotypes; for example, Bela Flek's jazz banjo performances or the Kronos Quartet's *Pieces of Africa* recording shows how traditions mix in interesting ways. Post information on concerts or festivals that help students move "outside the box." Ask your local CD retailer for posters from recent releases, or ask students to display interesting visual materials from the Internet.

Above all, demonstrate an attitude of accessibility: It's not just buildings or rooms that can be inaccessible to people with disabilities. Find ways to make your program more accessible; that includes thinking about the students, their parents, and the audience (Thompson, 1996). Take your ensemble to perform at institutions where people might not usually be able to go to concerts, such as a retirement home or school for people with severe disabilities. Provide an interpreter for deaf/hearing impaired listeners at your concerts, and ask the interpreter to sign for at least some of the choral selections. Last but not least, recruit young players for your program from all classes. Students with disabilities may be mainstreamed into music class, or special education students may have their own separate general music class. A "special needs" student might not receive much encouragement to try music, and yet that student might be very talented or interested in music. It's worth our time to see.

This article has attempted to point out a few instrumental "success stories" and show how we might bring those examples forward to our students. Certainly there are wonderful vocal "success stories" to which we might point as well. As we strive to motivate young musicians, we can expect to see increasingly diverse experiences and expectations. By building solid musical and social values, through many resources and strategies, we continue to reach and motivate more young people all the time.

References

Abeles, H. F & Porter, S.Y. (1978). The sex-stereotyping of musical instruments. *Journal of Research in Music Education, 26*, 65–75.

Fortney, P. M., Boyle, J. D., & DeCarbo, J. J. (1993). A study of middle school band students' instrument choices. *Journal of Research in Music Education, 41*, 28–39.

Hamann, D. L., & Walker, L. M. (1993). Music teachers as role models for African American students. *Journal of Research in Music Education, 41*, 303–314.

Hickman, J. W. (1994). *Magnificent Mendez*. Tempe, AZ: Summit Books.

Ostleitner, El & Simek, U. (1994). *Carole Dawn Reinhart: Aspects of career.* Vienna: WUV-Universitatsverlag, Berggasse.

Thompson, K. (1996). How accessible are your concerts? *Teaching Music, 4* (2), 33–34.

Vogel, L. (1989). Portraits: Evelyn Glennie (interview). *Modern Drummer, 13* (5), 46–50.

Walsh, M. (1994). A different drummer. *Time, 43* (12), 73.

Zervoudakes, J. & Tanur, J. (1994). Gender and musical instruments: Winds of change? *Journal of Research in Music Education, 42*, 58–67.

This article first appeared in the Winter 2001 issue of California's CMEA Magazine. *Reprinted by permission.*

Music Education for the Deaf and Hearing-Handicapped

Timothy J. Brown

It was my first day of teaching in a new building. The bell rang, the class shuffled out, and the next class came in. Along with the students, a woman whom I did not yet know came into my classroom. I introduced myself as the new music teacher and asked if I could help her. She said no, explaining that she was the interpreter. I asked, rather confused, "Interpreter for what?" She answered, pointing, "for those two deaf kids over there." That's how I was introduced to teaching music to mainstreamed deaf and hearing-handicapped children. (In all fairness, I should point out that I was already aware that my last class of the day would be composed entirely of hearing- handicapped students. However, I was unaware that these same children would also be mainstreamed in many of my other classes.)

Music in the Education of the Deaf and Hearing Handicapped

Teaching music to the deaf is not a new topic. In her February 1985 *Music Educators Journal* article, "Music for the Deaf," Alice-Ann Darrow refers to an 1848 case study by William Wolcott Turner and David Ely Bartlett. The Illinois School for the Deaf had a band for its students from 1923 to 1942 (Sheldon 1997). More recently, Eugenia Bulawa Walczyk described her experiences as an elementary school general music teacher (Walczyk 1993), as does Paul Gouge at the secondary school level (Gouge 1997). Sheila Gaskell, a private music teacher, has written about her successes teaching a deaf piano pupil (Gaskell 1997).

To some, music in the education of the deaf and hearing handicapped may on the surface seem to be a fruitless pursuit. After all, why teach them a subject which they lack, or only partially possess, the physical capability to perceive? Does one also teach blind children to paint? Many factors are to be considered when discussing this topic, including philosophical reasoning for having music as part of the curriculum of a deaf or hearing-handicapped child, the nature and amount of hearing loss (which varies from child to child), the degree to which each child will be able to use music in his/her life, and modifications to a usual teaching routine that need to be made to accommodate these students. Herein I shall address some of these concerns. This article, however, is not intended to provide a "recipe" for all music educators working with deaf and hearing-handicapped students.

Philosophy

A search of texts for training music educators, even those texts written for teachers dealing with special learners, reveals that, with some exceptions, literature on the topic of hearing loss has for the most part been limited. (One notable exception is a text by Atterbury, 1990.) Included in this body of literature are treatises on various physical and emotional challenges, often borrowed from the closely related field of music therapy. However, seldom does one encounter information about deaf and hearing-handicapped students. In most texts on music and special education, the topic is not adequately dealt with. There are few resources available to music teachers who have students with some form of hearing loss, no matter its severity and no matter the learning situation, be it an occasional mainstreamed student or an entire section of a music class for hearing-handicapped students. Therefore, there has also been very little available information about philosophical considerations about the inclusion of music in the education of these students.

The spirit of Public Law No. 94-142, passed in 1975 by the United States Congress, suggests the inclusion of music in the education of all students. The law reads, in part,

> Each school system shall take steps to ensure that its handicapped children have available to them the same variety of educational programs and services available to nonhandicapped children served by the school, including art, music, industrial arts, [and] consumer and vocational education. (United States Statutes at Large, 1977)

While this governmental mandate does little in the way of providing justification specifically for music in the education of deaf and hearing-handicapped students, it does address the broader issue of special education and the premise that all children have a right to equal and appropriate education. It is from this premise that music is included in the curriculum of the deaf and hearing handicapped, although the deaf community sometimes views this as an imposition of "hearing values" on them (Stewart 1990).

It is, however, appropriate to examine this issue beyond the level of the law itself. The merging of the hearing-handicapped population and music will then seem less rigid and lose the flavor of mandate. It seems more likely that teachers will be able to structure the learning environment in the most effective (and least restrictive) manner possible.

Relevance of Music to Hearing-Handicapped Students

When I was first assigned to teach the deaf and hearing-handicapped students, I was somewhat at a loss. I had not studied formally in either of my degree programs, or even informally on my own, music education for the deaf. I felt ill-prepared at best. I know only a smattering of sign language (my college choir had signed a song at the close of each of its concerts) and felt a great deal of anxiety. Much of my anxiety stemmed from lack of information and from popular myths. A central philosophical question for me was how can these students use music in their lives? My examination of that question has seemed to help resolve some of the dilemma because it has helped me to understand the place of music in the educational program.

Some educators have examined the role of music as it pertains to life in general in the population at large. If one examines the so-called "real-life" uses of music for nonchallenged peoples, then refocuses on potential real-life uses of music for the deaf and hearing handicapped, it becomes simpler to provide the most relevant and appropriate music education in the least restrictive environment.

Considering the uses and relevance of music for everyone is perhaps the easier of the two tasks. While there is probably no easily definable, discernible "list" to ponder, there are three central, recurring ideas. Human involvement in musical activities can be classified variously as (1) performance, including singing, playing instruments, and dance; (2) listening, including live and recorded performance; or (3) composing, including informal activities such as creating sound compositions, as well as the creation of formal, notated works (Regelski 1980). Deaf and hearing-handicapped people also participate in these activities to various degrees relative to their circumstances. In their own ways, deaf and hearing-handicapped children can perform music, listen to music, and compose music. The task of the educator becomes assessing each student to determine the most appropriate, effective musical activities.

One likely aspect of music to be used by the deaf is rhythm. Common games of the deaf are predicated upon it. Football plays at Gallaudet University, a college for the deaf, are called using various rhythms on a large bass drum whose vibrations the players can feel. Ken Walker of the Denver Broncos uses a similar system involving the use of rhythm at the professional football level. Since not all deaf children will become football players using only a narrow aspect of music in their lives, it is important to look more closely at the world of the deaf and ascertain what "musical" activities are used there.

Paul Gouge advocates using activities in the music classroom which involve the whole body (Gouge 1990). Other common musical activities of the deaf include motion and rhythm through watching and imitating, creating "sound" compositions, and some vocalizing and singing. Some can even match pitch when feeling the vibrations of an instrument or a singer's throat. The social aspect of music as an activity done with one's peers is also very important. A five-year-old hearing-handicapped student of mine seemed not to enjoy a self-contained music class for the deaf, but when we tried mainstreaming her (with an interpreter) in a kindergarten class, she had a wonderful time with her friends. She participated more fully in class, and even vocalized on some of the songs. Many deaf students enjoy singing and signing songs (Darrow 1985; Knapp 1980). Hearing students can learn to sign with their deaf peers and, in my experience, many have chosen to do so. Gouge (1990) describes a music club he sponsored for deaf secondary school students who were involved in singing and signing, and who also wrote their own songs.

Assessment

Degree of Hearing Loss

A factor in the determination of appropriate and effective musical activities is the degree and nature of hearing loss. There are varying degrees of hearing loss one may encounter. Chances are, we all have worked with students who have a slight amount of hearing loss. These students can still participate in musical activities with little modification. Students at the other end of the spectrum may have been profoundly deaf from birth. They may have extremely limited or no experience with sound.

Some of the students I have worked with are in yet a different category, since they have residual hearing which can be stimulated through personal amplification. Regarding these children, Graham and Beer (1980) state, "Where the hearing loss is only mild or moderate, the child should be given every opportunity to use whatever residual hearing is available in regular music education classes." Personal amplification generally refers to hearing aids. Some of my students use a system with phonic ears, an FM frequency connected to their own personal amplification. This system can also be used in a group situation, and the instructor can use a clip-on microphone. For greater benefit to the child, the music teacher can stand near the sound source, be it stereo speaker or piano, or actually clip the microphone there.

Still others may have had hearing at one time, but lost their hearing through disease or accident (e.g., spinal meningitis, brain trauma, etc.). Darrow (1985) states, "Only a small percentage of hearing-impaired individuals do not hear at all. Their greatest difficulty is in hearing well enough to develop speech and language." Audiograms can contain valuable information about what range of pitches at which dynamic levels can be heard. (One of my students cannot hear my soprano recorder, but can hear pitches on the piano below middle C.)

Language Abilities

A second factor is the "language" ability of the student. This ability is often influenced by the degree and time of onset of hearing loss. It is essential for the educator to consider this when determining how to communicate with the student, or when selecting songs for the class. Is he/she able to process English (or another language)? Some students experience a delay in their language abilities because their environment provided no input for them—they may have been unable to hear, but also did not develop language abilities because no one communicated with them. In an article written for *Music Educators Journal*, Fahey and Birkenshaw (1972) stressed this point when they stated, "The deaf child who is born profoundly deaf must have several years of highly specialized training before he has acquired the ability to communicate using language comparable to that of a normal five-year-old child."

What language skills exist? Is the student at the level of a three-year old learning to "speak" and read or identify letters, or can he/she comprehend sign language or read lips with sufficient proficiency to understand and be understood at approximately the same level as the peers with whom he/she may be mainstreamed? This may depend a great deal on the home environment. Deaf students who have used sign language from birth or from the onset of hearing loss typically have more advanced processing abilities. Does he/she have the ability to use the voice, or will he/she (and the teacher) need a sign-language interpreter? I have worked with one student with residual hearing who came to music classes with no interpreter. She is able to lip-read quite well, and for those times when she doesn't understand, she can sign with hearing classmates, several of whom have become fluent in sign through years of having these students mainstreamed in their classes.

The so-called whole-language approach used by many elementary-school teachers further compounds the language deficit many deaf and hearing-handicapped students may have. This approach includes the use of chants and songs to develop language skills. In a hearing population, the children have a common base of cultural literacy through the "casual" acquisition of experiences, including rote songs. These experiences, songs included, are not as readily accessible to the deaf. There are teachers who use these songs and chants in their self-contained classrooms for the deaf, but these are not necessarily learned in the same casual manner as they would be on the playground with hearing children.

Modifications

There are modifications to the "normal" teaching routine to be made depending on these factors. Included first are modifications to philosophy and traditional definitions of music. Music to the hearing population is not the same as it is in the deaf or hearing-impaired population. A hearing person, when asked to think of music, may imagine a Beethoven symphony; a profoundly deaf eight-year-old may think of music as the social activity of unison signing or playing rhythmic games with classmates.

As a result, the same listening lesson that hearing students may greatly enjoy and grow from may prove a disaster with our same deaf eight-year-old, who lacks the physical ability to perceive the sound and the language abilities to either understand the goals behind the listening or to communicate during the discussion of it. Such an activity clearly falls outside the expected in-life musical behaviors of the student and is unrealistic. Here, the definition of listening needs to be reconsidered. Provided the student has the sign language abilities, and provided the music has a "program" or text, listening for that child can amount to watching an interpreter. Some deaf adults, however, have told me they find this sort of visualization boring after a few minutes. To them, it sometimes seems as if everyone is speaking very slowly.

Another factor to be considered is appropriate placement of the hearing-handicapped student in the educational system. Two ways of dealing with special learners developed as a result of Public Law 94-142: mainstreaming, and the Individualized Education Program (termed Individualized Action Plan in some states). For some students, the self-contained classroom of hearing-handicapped children will be the least restrictive environment; for others, learning can take place more effectively when the student is mainstreamed in the hearing population. The IAP or IEP is a tool to assess and document the needs of each child to determine the scope and nature of his/her learning program. Consulting with the special-education faculty is imperative.

School administrations should also be prepared to make modifications. These might include allocating budgetary funds for the procurement of special equipment, such as electronic keyboards which can be connected to personal amplification, and providing training for the faculty and staff in deaf awareness and sign language. Interpreters should be provided at concerts and school assemblies as well as in class. Fostering of awareness of hearing students and development of their sign-language skills should also be undertaken.

Conclusion

In 1984, the Chamber Singers of the State University of New York College and School of Music at Fredonia were touring Great Britain. The group has traditionally signed "The Lord Bless You and Keep You" by John Rutter at the close of each concert. A deaf woman was in attendance at a concert, and burst into tears upon seeing this piece performed. She had never before seen a choir sign. Seeing each person sign with the choir in unison or with his/her section helped her understand something of the nature of music.

It is important to include music in the curricula of deaf and hearing-handicapped students and for music teachers to have the skills to teach these students. These students can and do use music in their lives, and should have the opportunity to learn this art form.

References

Abeles, Harold F., et al. 1984. *Foundations of music education.* New York: Schirmer Books.

Atterbury, Betty W. 1990. *Mainstreaming exceptional learners in music.* Englewood Cliffs, N.J.: Prentice-Hall.

Darrow, Alice-Ann. 1985. Music for the deaf. *Music Educators Journal* 71: 33–35.

Darrow, Alice-Ann. 1993. The role of music in deaf culture: Implications for music educators. *Journal of Research in Music Education* 41: 93–110.

Fahey, Joan Dahms, and Lois Birkenshaw. 1972. Bypassing the ear: The perception of music by feeling and touch. *Music Educators Journal* 58: 44–49.

Gaskell, Sheila. 1997. Teaching a deaf pupil. *Music Teacher* 76: 20–21.

Gouge, Paul. 1990. Music and profoundly deaf students. *British Journal of Music Education* 7: 279–281.

Graham, Richard M., and Alice S. Beer. 1980. *Teaching music to the exceptional child: A handbook for mainstreaming*. Englewood Cliffs, N.J.: Prentice-Hall.

Grayson, John. 1972. A playground of musical sculpture. *Music Educators Journal* 58: 50–54.

Grimley, Terry. 1997. Opera and the deaf audience. *Music Teacher* 76: 12–13.

Knapp, Ruth Ann. 1980. A choir for total communication. *Music Educators Journal* 66: 54–55.

Regelski, Thomas R. 1980. *Teaching general music.* New York: Schirmer Books.

Sheldon, Deborah. 1997. The Illinois School for the Deaf Band. *Journal of Research in Music Education* 45: 580–600.

Sposato, M. A. 1982. Implications of maximal exploitation of residual hearing on curriculum planning in music education for hearing-impaired children. Ed.D. dissertation, State University of New York at Buffalo.

Spotlight: Focus on young singers—Adey Grummet. 1998. *Choir and Organ* 6: 23.

U.S. Congress. 1977. Public laws and the 94th Congress, First session. *United States Statutes at Large 89: 773.* Washington, D.C.: U.S. Government Printing Office.

Walczyk, Eugenia Bulawa. 1993. Music instruction and the hearing impaired. *Music Educators Journal* (July): 42–44.

Williams, Helen. 1965. The value of music to the deaf. *Music Journal* 42.

The author wishes to give special thanks to his students; teachers of the hearing handicapped and sign language interpreters of the Denver Public Schools: Susan Dickinson, Rose Consoer, Marty Bleidt, Ruth Ryll, Cathy Adelman, Moe Keller; Galen Darrough, University of Northern Colorado; Janet Montgomery, University of Colorado at Boulder.

This article first appeared in the Spring 2000 issue of the Colorado Music Educator. *Reprinted by permission.*

A Small Warm Hand: The Reason We Teach

Esther D'Agrosa

I'll tell you something
I think you'll understand
Then I'll say that something
I want to hold you hand.
—John Lennon and Paul McCartney

It was Friday morning, yet again. The special education class from Longfellow Elementary School would be coming at 10:00 a.m. as usual. It promised to be a busy day and I was already tired from a busier than usual week. With certainty, the children arrived at the door at the appointed time, wearing winter jackets and good spirits. During this semester, college students in the elementary methods class and I grew to love the once-a-week opportunity to work with these children.

The lesson of the day—teach the "Jingle Bells Dance," a circle dance with steps accessible to these students, and fun to do in December. The process began. I stepped inside the circle, modeled the first four beats, stepped back into the circle and invited the students to repeat the steps.

As I stepped back into the circle, I felt the warmth of a small hand in mine, and glanced down at the smiling face of Brenna. The dance teaching process continued as usual, and each time I stepped back to the circle, that small hand reached for mine. The dance was completed and the class enjoyed performing it together.

We bid goodbye to the children, and the day marched on. The events of the morning faded in the distance of deadlines to keep and problems to solve.

Sleep that night came quickly for me. It was only in the middle of the night that I awoke, with the remembrance of that little hand reaching for mine. Suddenly it became apparent to me that I had overlooked the most significant moment of the day—and the very reason I love teaching so much. Teaching is all about connections. The connections between student and teacher, student and student, student and content, and student and teacher to the larger world, are the essence of our daily work. My revelation in the middle of the night was that I must always work to keep that centrality uppermost each day.

And so I encourage you. The days are filled with things to do, deadlines, concerts and informances to prepare, paper work and more paper work, meetings, and what else?—perhaps lunch duty!

In the midst of all the flurry of activity, take time to feel that hand in yours—to remember the touching moments you have encountered with your students. I am quite sure it will warm your heart and enrich your teaching, as Brenna's hand did for me.

This article first appeared in the April 2002 issue of the Iowa Music Educator. *Reprinted by permission.*

Differentiating Instruction in the Music Classroom

Ruth Ann Debrot

The term "differentiating instruction" means to teach all aspects of student learning and skill levels in one classroom. This includes students with learning disabilities, visual disabilities, behavioral disorders, hearing disabilities, the physically challenged, and students with higher learning potential. That can seem extremely overwhelming when you stop and think about it! However, most classes will need adaptations for one or two students at a time and as you will note, many of the strategies that work for one student may be applied to all students who need differentiated instruction techniques.

There are some general guidelines for all students with special needs. The first is to get information about each student by talking to teachers, parents, counselors, and the students themselves. Become familiar with particular disabilities and avoid preconceptions about what students can or cannot do. Often, students who are not successful in the academic classroom can achieve great success in a music class that is structured for that very purpose.

Keeping an organized classroom free from distractions and keeping directions simple and direct will help all children, and especially disabled students who tend toward sensory overload. Establishing lesson routines such as a beginning song and ending song can be comforting for children who need structure.

Research has shown we all have different learning styles. Some of us learn best through the auditory mode. Others learn by visual mode or kinesthetic mode. The most important principle for lesson preparation is that materials are presented in as many modes as possible. The most effective music program for most children is a hands-on, participatory program that emphasizes varied activities such as movement, instruments, rhythm, speech, sound exploration, melody, and dance.

Students who are learning disabled process information differently than others. However, the term implies that the basic capacity to learn is intact. Often these students are bright but have difficulty learning to read. Some famous people in this category are Albert Einstein, Nelson Rockefeller, Leonardo DaVinci and Thomas Edison. There are some strategies for learning-disabled students, who may vary greatly in the way that their brain is able to process information.

Learning-disabled students who have difficulty reading may struggle with written musical concepts. Preparing simple visual charts will help understanding of musical concepts. Music textbooks contain a lot of information, but they may be confusing for the learning disabled student by providing too much information at one time. Using color helps highlight key concepts. (Example: *do* = blue, *re* = red, *mi* = green). Rhythm patterns may be learned more easily if they are isolated into small pieces on a large visual. Phrases may be indicated by a change in color. Introducing literacy concepts in small chunks during the lesson may be less frustrating to the learning disabled student who may be fatigued easily because of processing difficulty. Use repetition (drill) but present material in different ways so that students have time to absorb concepts.

Students who are visually impaired may be wonderful musicians because they have developed superior auditory skills to compensate for their eyesight. These students can certainly learn songs by rote and echoing patterns. They can also play rhythm instruments without problems. Movement may be challenging for these students if there is not enough open space. A "movement partner" may be helpful. Remember to read aloud any information that is presented visually. Today there are large-print scores available for piano, voice, organ, strings, brass, woodwind, guitars, and recorders. If the vision impairment is severe, it may be helpful to give a "tour" of the room so that the child is familiar with the location of materials.

Behavioral disorders have various causes and may be combined with a learning disability, adding additional frustration for the student. Some students may be aggressive and have difficulty focusing on a task. The causes of aggressive behavior may be social (dysfunctional family, environment) or genetic (chemical imbalance). Other students may be anxious and withdrawn. Withdrawn behavior can also be caused by social (neglect or abuse) or biological causes.

Music class can be a positive force for these children. Routine and structure can be comforting for them. Though it may be difficult, remain calm and don't lose your temper. Begin and end with a familiar song and maintain a routine from lesson to lesson. Aggressive students may not be able to maintain focus for long so vary the drill by playing or singing with different articulation and dynamics. Props, such as puppets, may be used to give directions in a nonthreatening way. Songs or games that contain directions may be helpful for children who normally have difficulty following verbal directions or who have authority issues. Children who are withdrawn seek security and find comfort in repetition. They tend to respond well to 3/4 and 6/8 meter.

Students with a moderate or mild hearing disability are often good students but have difficulty developing language and regularly see a speech and language pathologist. These students have strong visual, kinesthetic, and tactile modes of learning. Face students when talking so they will able to read your lips and provide as many visual cues as possible. Sing songs in a lower key (anything above C over middle C is too high to detect) so these students can understand the words better. Use instruments and movement so that these students will have an opportunity for success in something other than singing. Singing may help these children with their speech and language skills so give thought to vocabulary and the understanding of everyday activities when selecting song literature.

There are a variety of physical disabilities. These students can also achieve success in the music classroom. Health problems such as cystic fibrosis, heart trouble, asthma, diabetes, or even AIDS are most often controlled medically; however one should use caution not to overdo any movement that can cause fatigue or shortness of breath. Epilepsy can also be controlled medically. Cerebral palsy is a non-progressive disability and has varying degrees of severity. The main problem with cerebral palsy is muscle control which does not affect intellectual ability in most cases. Muscular dystrophy students may need a lot of emotional support. Their condition is irreversible and will only get worse.

Singing is a good activity for these students. It helps breathing and lung control. Instruments such as Orff instruments can be adapted by removing bars so that any note played will be correct. Orff instruments also fit nicely onto a wheelchair tray. Adaptive mallets are also available as are Velcro straps for hands drums and other percussion instruments. There is even a one-handed recorder. A physical disability does not mean a lesser interest in music. Listening and responding to recorded music may be a great source of comfort and interest for children who are physically unable to move and/or play their own music.

On the other side of the learning spectrum, there are students with higher learning potential. These students cannot be identified by IQ scores alone. Giftedness in music transcends such measurement. Musicality cannot be measured by one's ability to read music either, or musicians such as Stevie Wonder could not have made a career in music. Perhaps it is correct then to define this student as persistent, responsible, and highly motivated. Not all of these children are performers either, as one might think. Hence, there are those musicians who become historians and researchers of music.

To address the needs of higher learning potential students, we can offer a variety of activities including acceleration (offering assignments that allow students to go to differing levels), enrichment (extra lessons such as on Saturdays at a conservatory), technological instruction (computer programs that offer composition, research, or theory), and perhaps a mentor for the student. Maintaining the integrity of performing ensembles and offering advanced ability ensembles can address the needs of those students who prefer concentrating on the performing arts.

Differentiating lesson plans will address the needs of all learners in the classroom if you recall that every student has a learning style that is unique. Presenting material aurally, visually, tactilely, and orally will insure that you connect with the varied learning styles for all students. The use of speech, movement, instruments, and singing in each lesson will insure that each child feels some degree of success. Orff arrangements can offer a variety of skill levels in one piece. Differing levels of achievement may be addressed by having some children play complex patterns while others play a simple steady beat and some merely sing. Offering older students a choice of assignments with different criteria can challenge gifted students while giving other students in the class the chance to be successful as well.

Mainstreaming is now commonplace in public education. More children are being recognized as having disabilities, and they are in our classes. Each of these children has the potential to love music and feel good about music. It's up to us, as informed educators, to make our lessons as effective as possible by using a multisensory approach that is child centered and addresses the learning needs of all students.

Bibliography

Atterbury, Betty W. *Mainstreaming Exceptional Learners in Music*, Englewood Cliffs: Prentice Hall, 1990.

Birkenshaw, Lois. *Music For Fun, Music For Learning*, third edition, St. Louis: MMB Music, Inc. 1982.

Birkenshaw-Fleming, Lois. *Music For All: Teaching Music to*

People With Special Needs, Toronto: Gordon V. Thompson Music, 1993.

Sample Lesson Plan with Modifications

Grade 6

Title: "Better Late Than Never"

Concepts: Rhythm notation, pitch notation, mallet technique, ABA form, rondo form, improvisation

Process

1. Echo-clap rhythms of the rhyme (auditory preparation).
2. Have the class echo the poem. (Provide a visual of the poem. Use color to indicate patterns and phrases.) Vary repetition by using soft/loud/high/low vocal textures.
3. Read the rhythm of the poem, provide a visual. (*Ti-ti, ti-ti, ti-ti*, rest, etc.)
4. Identify patterns and phrase structure.
5. Transfer the rhythms to body percussion and then unpitched percussion.
6. Practice saying and playing the rhyme in rondo form.
7. Transfer the rhythm to pitched instruments. Play the rhythm on one note before moving on to the pitches. Work on mallet technique.
8. Echo-sing the correct pitches for auditory preparation.
9. Show pitches on a visual—sing the pitches.
10. Play the pitches on barred instruments.
11. Continue this process until all parts are accumulated.
12. Create ABA form by playing rhyme for A and allowing the group to improvise on the rhyme for a B section. (F pentatonic scale will insure successful improvisation.)
13. When the students are comfortable with the improvisation, invite solos and make an extended rondo form.

ti-ti *ti-ti* *ti-ti*(rest)
Better late than never.
ti-ti *ti-ti* *ti-ti*(rest)
Better late than never.
ti-ti *ta* *ti-ti* *ta*
Better late, better late,
ti-ti *ti-ti* *ta ta*
Better late than never.

This article first appeared in the Winter 2002 issue of the Massachusetts Music News. *Reprinted by permission.*

Abraham and Frank

Richard A. Disharoon

October 20, 1998, started out as another normal day at Pikesville High School. The Music for Life class would begin as usual at 9:35 a.m. Students had been using the Boomwhackers to create rhythm patterns and were required to notate their pattern. Their progress had been informally assessed in previous lessons. Today, students would use a new set of guidelines for creating a pattern. A formal assessment as well as a self-assessment of their work would let us know if we could move on.

Several thoughts ran through my head as I mentally prepared for the class. I expected that I would need to remind Jacob of the Boomwhacker Rules established by the class: no sword fighting, don't hit anyone on the head, etc. I wondered if this would be the day when this very nice heterogeneous group of 26 kids in grades 9–12 who had been lacking in enthusiasm would "come alive." So far, I had failed to do anything that turned them on. They just sat politely day after day working quietly to attain the objectives of the lesson.

The heterogeneous grouping of this class was very broad, encompassing ability levels from special education through gifted and talented as well as students in grades 9 through 12. One of the real challenges of this class was to allow the two special education students enough time to complete tasks while keeping the G/T students occupied with additional meaningful activities. One of those meaningful activities was to have them, along with other students with good musical background, mentor other students, including the special education students.

They were, however, reluctant to help Abraham, a freshman special education student who was very slow. Abraham had been a very premature baby. I knew that he could "get it," but he required much more patience on my part than most students with a learning problem. Abraham's situation was complicated by being socially unaccepted by the other students. It didn't help that Abraham dressed in traditional Orthodox Jewish garb: white dress shirt open at the collar, black pants, socks, and shoes. And, of course, a yarmulke.

Abraham's parents had done a beautiful job of rearing him. He was eager to learn. His hand was always in the air to answer or to ask questions. The other students would snicker at his comments.

Eventually, the snickering was stopped by the glances I directed at the offending students.

The other special education student was Frank. Frank was big enough to have been a lineman on the football team. Instead, he was a severely emotionally disturbed senior. I knew that my windowless room contributed to his lack of class participation. He was almost totally dysfunctional on cloudy days. In a sense, it was always cloudy in Music Room 1. He often didn't turn in assignments until I gave personal encouragement. On most days, Frank was passively uncooperative.

But I had discovered that Frank really had an intense interest in music. He was knowledgeable about the piano keyboard and writing notation. On several days early in the year, he had stayed around after class to ask about the keyboard. He hoped to save enough money from his job to buy one. Then, he would go off to work with the custodial staff for the rest of the day.

And so, my mental preparation for class on October 20th included thoughts about how I would get Abraham and Frank through this formal assessment lesson.

As always, the class came in slowly. I showed them the transparency with the objective for the lesson and reminded them that violation of the Boomwhacker Rules would result in handing in their Boomwhackers and scheduling a private session at 7 a.m. Then, I asked for volunteers to mentor students who were having trouble notating rhythms. As usual, no one volunteered to mentor Abraham. As the class set to work, I pondered how to spend adequate time with Abraham so he would have a good assessment and still give time to all the other students. I asked a specific student to mentor Abraham. More reluctance. Then, I heard a voice say, "I'll do it." To my surprise, Frank was volunteering to mentor Abraham. I knew Frank could do it, so with a few words of encouragement, the two set to work.

As I moved around the room helping other students, I kept a watchful eye on Abraham and Frank. Based on previous experience, my one worry was that Frank would loose patience, throw down the Boomwhackers, and say, "I'm not doing this anymore."

The Boomwackers are hollow plastic tubes of varying lengths which enable them to produce pitch. Each pitch of the two octave range is a different color. Out of the corner of my eye, I saw Frank make sure that they both had the same color Boomwhacker in their left and right hands.

Frank asked Abraham to play a rhythm. His first uncoordinated attempt produced almost nothing recognizable as a rhythm. Patiently, Frank asked Abraham to try again. Abraham's second attempt was more successful, producing a rhythm which was immediately notated by Frank. Then they set about playing this rhythm.

I could hardly take my eyes off of them. Soon, I became aware that other students were watching as well. In spite of my encouragement to continue working, a few still stopped to watch. By having Abraham imitate him as he played each note of the pattern, Frank lead Abraham successfully through the entire pattern. If Abraham made a mistake, Frank would say "No Abraham, that's not it. Watch me. Let's try again." He never raised his voice. I marveled at Frank's patience.

I didn't want to stop this wonderful moment, but the end of class time was approaching and the students knew that they would be called on to play their patterns. As it was, I knew I hadn't left enough time for all to play. That was ok. Tomorrow was another day. What was happening between Frank and Abraham was more important.

As usual, when I asked for a volunteer to play his/her pattern, no one moved. And then Frank said, "Abraham and I will play his pattern." It seemed to take forever, but no one in the room moved. All eyes were riveted on Frank and Abraham. The only sounds in the room were Frank's quiet voice of encouragement and Abraham's eventual plunk of the Boomwhacker. Playing the pattern seemed to take forever. When they were finished, the class burst into applause. Abraham beamed. Frank grinned. What a moment!

But there was more to come. I asked Abraham to assess his performance. He replied, "I was able to do this because my friend Frank helped me." By this time, tears were streaming down my face. I was speechless. Thank God the bell rang.

Frank continued to help Abraham for the next several days. It was wonderful to watch. Frank allowed himself a wry smile when I congratulated him on his work as a mentor. And Abraham had never smiled so much. From that moment on, no one every refused to mentor Abraham.

Frank went from an "E" second quarter when he turned in very little work to an "A" for the fourth quarter and a "B" for the year. By the end of the year, with the help of mentors, Abraham refined his coordination skills and was able to play some tunes on the electronic keyboard. He earned a "B" for the year.

Although October 20th didn't start out differently from any other day, it ended up holding one of the most significant moments of my career in education. Although music content was learned that day, a more important life lesson was learned by the entire class. I was proud that it happened in my class.

This article first appeared in the January/February 2000 issue of the Maryland Music Educator. *Reprinted by permission.*

Attention Deficits and the Choral Rehearsal

Patrick K. Freer

"Ugh." Flinch. "That term just sends shivers up my spine." What does the mere mention of the term Attention Deficit Disorder bring to your mind? I quickly polled some colleagues and came up with comments ranging from "empathy" and "teacher creativity" to "cop-out" and "dumbing down the curriculum."

A great deal of energy has been spent in recent years trying to meet the needs of every kid in our classrooms—especially those labeled with ADD. What has emerged is a large body of recommendations which mostly reaffirm what we've been doing for a long time, particularly in the choral rehearsal.

The work of Dr. Melvin Levine has spurred a greater understanding of students with learning difficulties. A physician with a profound dedication to enabling each student to understand his or her educational strengths and weaknesses, Dr. Levine has influenced the work of the entire field of special education. Implications of his work are being implemented most directly in specific schools throughout the state, including Clinton Township, the New Grange School in Princeton, and the East Windsor schools. The following article incorporates the main points of Dr. Levine's contributions to our understanding of attention.

What has become apparent is that terms such as Attention Deficit Disorder or Attention Deficit Hyperactivity Disorder are misleading in the sense that they are broad terminologies. The real question becomes what area of attention is causing the difficulty. Determining the area in which students (or we ourselves) have a weakness helps us understand the specific challenges we have when tailoring our efforts to meet individual needs. No longer are we dealing with an ADD student, but we may be dealing with a task much more concrete and manageable. And, if we are able to identify a student's attention problems, we will probably recognize areas of attention which are strengths for that student—for rarely will a student have difficulties with each area of "attention." We can then make some decisions about our instruction: do we "bypass" the area of difficulty, or do we deal directly with that area of attention which is resulting in less than optimal performance and/or achievement in our rehearsals?

All students can benefit from the adapting of lessons to promote greater attentional skills. And, you might find that you have fun utilizing some of these strategies within every rehearsal!

The Attention Controls

There are three primary factors concerning our ability to focus and pay attention:

I. The Processing Controls

The processing controls correspond to how our brains receive information. These processing controls can be viewed as five factors—each of which may be a source of strength or an area of weakness in a student.

1. **Saliency Determination.** There is a ton of information bombarding a student each moment of the day: the color of the walls, the notes played on the piano, the information printed in the choral octavo, the bug crawling across the floor, the bird chirping outside the window. A chief responsibility of a well-balanced processing control is to determine which of these is the most important, or "salient."

   Cues: high distractibility (visual, auditory, tactile, social, etc.)

   Strategies:

   a. Questioning techniques
      - "What do you think we should do now?"

   b. Substitute plans
      - Students design the day's rehearsal as if for a substitute.

   c. Listening and responding to audio recordings of rehearsals when given specific directions ("listen for the [a] vowel").

   d. Rehearsal ears
      - Students listen to and comment on a portion of rehearsal.

   e. Summary of accomplishments or assignments

2. **Depth of Processing.** This basically corresponds to how thoroughly information is understood. A multisensory approach to a piece

of information is likely to be retained by our minds more easily than something which is simply spoken aloud by a teacher. In the film "Dead Poets Society" there is a scene where the professor played by Robin Williams jumps up on a desk to make a point. Nobody is suggesting that you should invest in gymnastics training so that you can replace the solfège hand signals with whole body contortions, but it does suggest that information which is taught through more than one routine method has a greater chance of being understood deeply by students with attentional difficulties.

Cues: the student responds in superficial ways; exhibits excellent skill ability but careless errors; becomes bogged down in details

Strategies:

a. Clear directions with eye-to-eye contact

b. Use multiple methods of presenting materials:
- teacher vocal modeling
- color-coded music scores
- allowing students to "journal" about rehearsal
- isolate one concept at a time (breathing, vowels, line, etc.)

3. **Mental Activation**. No, this does not directly correspond to the amount of caffeine or sugar consumed at lunch. Rather, mental activation is related to how well a student draws upon prior knowledge to make sense of new information.

Cues: lack of interest, overuse of rote memory, lack of strategies for problem solving, boredom.

Strategies:

a. Editor (especially good when using a substantial text)
- Why did the composer choose to do this at this time?
- Would you have chosen something different

b. Biographer
- What happened in the poet's life just before this was written?

c. Use multiple methods of presenting materials

d. Use of imagery
- example: sports imagery whenever possible: spiraling football pass = long, ringing note; swimming = energy during a long phrase; figure skating jump = vocal energy before high note

4. **Focal Maintenance.** This term is pretty self-explanatory—the ability to maintain focus and concentration. This is the area we most commonly note as the attention span of a student.

Cues: a student simply stops concentrating.

Strategies:

a Timekeeper
- Keeping the teacher "on schedule" with rehearsal

b. Scribe
- Teacher outlines rehearsal on board, student checks-off when a part of the outline is accomplished.

c. Cooperative learning techniques:
- jigsawing
- think-pair-share
- prism concert

5. **Satisfaction Level**. For each situation, and at each moment of the day, a student makes a usually unconscious decision about whether that situation is satisfying or not. If so, attention will be given to the situation. If not, attention will go elsewhere—anywhere which is more satisfying to the student and somewhere which does not always particularly please the teacher!

Cues: student craves excitement or materials.

Strategies:

a. Vary the energy output of your teaching approach, using frequent modulations of vocal volume, physical location in the room, visual and aural support materials.

b. Vary the energy output required of the students, including physical location in the room. Give students something to do rather than simply sit and absorb information. Give students ordinary pipe cleaners to manipulate with their hands while you expect them to focus on learning and/or singing.

II. Mental Energy Control

Human brains need to regulate how much energy is expended on paying attention, and that regulation manifests itself in two major ways:

1. **Level of Alertness.**

Cues: yawning, stretching, trying to create "discomfort" in order to stay awake, inconsistent concentration, miss parts of the directions

Strategies:

a. Incorporate movement into rehearsal

b. Vary seating arrangements

c. Singing circles
- Divide students into groups (voice parts?) and sit in circles on the floor.

2. Level of Mental Effort

Cues: mental fatigue, trouble finishing homework or classwork, willing to succeed but lacking the "fuel" to sustain effort

Q: How unexciting or personally uninteresting can class be before the student loses the capacity to put forth and sustain effort?

A: Do everything possible to keep that student involved.

Strategies:

a. Limit rehearsal goals
- Work on just one phrase/page of each piece per rehearsal.

b. Breaks
- Allow students to stand or move around room.

c. Physical activity
- Keep the hands busy by giving something to hold, e.g., a pipe cleaner or a "koosh" ball.

d. Alert student when important information is coming by a physical touch on the shoulder or by saying, "Now listen very carefully ..."

e. Use imagery from student experience
- Singing is like riding horses. (You'll have to be creative!)

III. Production Controls

The ability of our brains to "output" information is also controlled by attention. There are five areas through which we can glimpse these attentional production controls.

1. Previewing. The ability to foresee potential outcomes.

Cues: like a photographer who doesn't use a viewfinder—doing the work but having no idea of what the results will be

Strategies:

a. Share rehearsal plans with your students

b. "What would happen if ..."
- we performed without piano?
- you stood frozen like a soldier for this phrase?
- you sang forte while the rest of your section sang piano?

c. Composer prediction
- Read text of a new piece, predict how the music will sound.
- Look at a page of new music, predict how the music will sound through noticing the expressive markings, etc.

d. Diagram a piece on the board

2. Facilitation and Inhibition. This control facilitates responses or actions which are desired and stops those which are not desired. You've probably experienced a student who, when asked the composer of Messiah could, along the road to saying "Handel," relate the entire story of King George standing, question aloud, "gee, I wonder if he had to go to the bathroom after sitting for three hours," relate that, "my mom sings that every Christmas and my sister got a Tickle-Me Elmo for Christmas last year, and I think that the frenzy over the Elmo dolls is part of a plot to kick out Ernie from the brotherhood of Sesame Street." Wow. And, you were only asking for "Handel." That student was unable to inhibit every extraneous bit of information which flowed through his mind as he thought about the answer.

Cues: impulsive, extraneous movement

Strategies:

a. Opposing teams
- Divide choir into two sections, rehearsing as usual, but alternating which group sings (even every other phrase).

b. Unusual conducting
- Take a familiar piece and insert unusual expressive items (ritardando, crescendo, staccato, etc.).

3. Tempo Control. Very simply, this concerns controlling the rate of speed and the pacing of actions. A weakness in tempo control is exhibited in students who work extraordinarily slowly or who rush to conclusions.

Cues: trouble thinking through consequences, hyperactivity

Strategies:

a. Timekeeper (see above)

b. Give activity outlets
- erasing the board, distributing music
- sorting through a pile of music which is in the corner, but only when student determines the need for activity
- allow kids to tap their thigh rather than the chair, etc.

4. Self-Monitoring. We might see a challenge in this area with students who are having difficulty detecting mistakes when singing a choral passage.

Cues: difficulty detecting mistakes, evaluating and interpreting feedback

Strategies:

a. Ask: "Did I (teacher) accomplish my goals for this rehearsal?"

b. Tape recorder

- assignment to sing a piece (or phrase) into a tape recorder and submit the tape when pleased with the result

c. Reviewer
- As at a newspaper, write a review of a video performance of a model choir.
- Write a review of a video performance of own choir.

5. **Reinforcement.** This is how we all learn from experience. A well-functioning Processing Control allows us to learn from our successes and failures and apply that knowledge at the next appropriate time. A student having difficulty with reinforcement will not be able to make those connections as readily.

Cues: students don't apply skills previously mastered.

Strategies:

a. Constantly encourage students to think about how to solve a problem. ("How did we dc this last time?")

b. Remain consistent. Use a variety of teaching techniques, but use each one in a consistent manner.

Each of these rehearsal strategies is possible and practical for any rehearsal situation even though each suggestion focuses on one area of attentional difficulties. Incorporating students with ADD or any attentional weakness need not be especially burdensome—particularly if you can find out the specific areas which are causing difficulty for the student. Check with the school psychologist or support committee for detailed help with a particular student.

This article first appeared in the March 1997 issue of New Jersey's Tempo. *Reprinted by permission.*

Evaluating Special Learners

Susan C. Gardstrom

One of the ongoing challenges we face as educators is how to best evaluate our students in music. Grading is a necessary aspect of what we do. Not only are we expected to provide periodic feedback about the quantity and quality of our students' performance to parents, colleagues, and administrators, but we ourselves need some means by which to measure changes—hopefully progress toward mastery—among the young musicians in our classrooms and ensembles.

The importance of evaluation can be magnified for those of us who teach special needs students. Many concerns emerge: How do we evaluate in a valid and reliable fashion? We may be faced with the dilemma of developing and implementing an evaluation system that upholds the standards and expectations of the school system in which we teach, yet one that allows for individual differences in ability. This is particularly evident in heterogeneous classrooms in which students demonstrate a wide range of cognitive, physical, and emotional or behavioral functioning. Furthermore, we may be asked to justify a unique grading system to others, including the regular education students in our classrooms and ensembles. Finally, we must address the possibility that we will be perceived by students and colleagues as lax or inequitable if we modify evaluative standards or procedures for our special needs students.

The purpose of this column is to provide the reader with some evaluative strategies for use with atypical students. Included here are both adaptations of traditional grading procedures and useful alternatives.

Traditional Grading

The most frequently used system of evaluation is the letter or numerical grade. Students are assigned a grade based on achievement of predetermined and, hopefully, clearly articulated criteria. This system, while perceived as valid and reliable, may not successfully accommodate your special needs students without modification. Some suggestions follow:

1. Group grading. The student participates in group experiences and is assigned a grade based on his contribution to the group process and product. Example: The student works cooperatively with two peers to create and perform a three-verse blues.

2. Project options. In this alteration, the student is provided a "menu" of task choices. Example: The student will complete two of the four projects offered in each of the following categories: improvisation, composition, vocal performance, instrumental performance.

3. Extra credit. The student has opportunities to improve a grade through completion of extra assignments related in content and scope. Example: The student designs and prepares a poster about the genre of music being studied.

4. Test options. Measurement through testing is modified to allow for a variety of learning styles.

This may include giving extra time for testing, allowing retesting or offering format options, such as oral and written measures. Example: The student is allowed to take a test home overnight and tape-record her musical and/or verbal answers.

5. Contract. The student and teacher form an individual contract at the start of the grading period. This contract specifies precise expectations for grade assignment. Example: The student and teacher agree that a grade of "B" involves completion of a musical and didactic presentation on the music of Mexico in addition to all requirements established for grades of "C."

6. Credit grades. All students are awarded the highest possible grade at the beginning of the period and must demonstrate certain knowledge, ability, or skills in order to maintain that grade.

Alternative to Traditional Evaluation

Where necessary and feasible, the following alternatives may be used to evaluate the achievements of our special learners in the music classroom.

1. Pass-fail. This system makes a clear distinction between acceptable and unacceptable musical achievement. Unlike letter or numerical systems, students are not rank-ordered.

2. Task-mastery. In this system, the student is expected to achieve a certain level of musical mastery. Tasks often are laid out in a sequential or developmental fashion and may be negotiated by the student and the teacher. Example: The student will accurately and independently play three assigned four-phrase melodies on the metallaphone using both hands.

3. Progress chart. The student or teacher keeps a chart or log of progress. It may be possible to document this in quantitative terms (e.g., in raw points or percentages).

The evaluation of students with special needs may be a complicated process. At times it may feel like an unnecessary burden. However, as music specialists, it is our responsibility not only to engage special needs students in meaningful active and receptive musical experiences, but to devise and implement a credible and equitable system to track and report their progress. An honest reflection of musical growth may ultimately motivate the student to excel in what we consider to be one of the most rewarding endeavors of this life.

This article first appeared in the May–June 2001 issue of Ohio's TRIAD. *Reprinted by permission.*

What's In A Name?

Susan C. Gardstrom

What's in a name? The answer to that question is *attitude*. The labels we use to describe people and events around us both affect and reflect our attitudes toward them. Labels are commonplace and unavoidable in educational settings. In special education, the labels we assign to learners are often useful in communicating with colleagues as well as necessary for determining the scope of services appropriate for a particular child and securing the necessary funding for those services (Darrow & White, 1998).

What labels do we use to describe the special learners in our classrooms and communities? Are we aware of the correct terminology for each of the different disability areas? Labels change frequently in response to factors such as public sentiment, advocacy, and legal action. It can be difficult to know what language is acceptable in conversations about children with disabling conditions. A few general guidelines follow.

First, we need not mention the disability at all, unless it is relevant to the topic at hand. For example, when talking about intonation among the clarinets in our beginning band, there is likely no reason to distinguish the student who has a visual impairment from the other players in the section.

If we need to use a label, though, it may help to remember this two-part axiom: (1) Make sure a person is present in the label, and (2) place the person first and the discriptor second. That is, rather than saying, "the learning disabled," (a reference to the disability category and not the individuals, or "the autistic boy," we ought to be using phrases such as "the children who have learning disabilities" and "the boy with autism." This terminology acknowledges that the student is first and foremost a human being—a person who just happens to have been born with or acquired a disability, just as another individual might have been born with red hair or acquired braces on their teeth. Finally, we ought to emphasize the capabilities of the learner rather than call attention to the deficits or differences. Although it may appear to be a subtle distinction, describing a student as a child who "uses an alternative communication device" conveys a much different and more positive attitude than referring to her as a girl who "cannot speak."

More detailed information about language relating to disabilities appears in "Sticks and Stones ... and Words CAN Hurt: Eliminating Handicapping Language." This is an excellent article which was written last year by Alice-Ann Darrow, PhD, MT-BC and Glen White, PhD. (See reference at bottom.)

For some time now, OMEA has used the label "special learners" to designate the children under our tutelage who have unique characteristics and needs. Let us continue to embody the compassion and respect this label suggests in all that we say or do on their behalf.

Reference

Darrow, A. A. & White, G. (1998). Sticks and Stones ... and Words CAN Hurt: Eliminating Handicapping Language. *Music Therapy Perspectives* 16(2). Silver Spring, MD: American Music Therapy Association.

This article first appeared in the December 1999–January 2000 issue of Ohio's TRIAD. *Reprinted by permission.*

Proactive Steps to Inclusion Placement in Music Class

Victoria S. Hagedorn

A topic of interest to many music educators is the placement or inclusion of special needs students in the general education music classroom. The "desire to include all students in the regular classroom has become more commonly known as the inclusive movement of full inclusion" (Wilson, 1996, p. 15). This movement is concerned with providing access to all special learners regardless of the severity or type of disability. However, "the vague parameters for this regulation have led to varying interpretations of the law by individual school districts" (Adamek, 1996, p. 9).

Goals of Inclusion

Inclusion offers the most independent setting for a special needs child. It is the "full time placement in the special education student's home district regular education system with chronological age grade placement" (Snell, 1996, p. 159). There, the student might be offered special educational services, either in pull-out or in-class situations. The child may also receive an adapted or regular curriculum with the possible help of a full-time or part-time aide (p.160).

Goals of inclusion include development of social skills for all school age groups, improvement of nondisabled students' attitudes toward special students, and development of positive relationships between these peer groups. Wilson (p.16) suggested that most professionals agree that there are benefits to be found in inclusion, such as: working toward improved interaction among professionals, better coordination of services for students, searching for effective and economical methods to serve these students, identifying special learners only when necessary, and supporting research leading to improved instruction for all students. However, there remain several areas of controversy about full inclusion: (1) Are fewer students receiving needed services as a result of integration and nonlabeling of students? (2) Does empirical evidence support the belief that inclusion actually promotes greater socialization and academic skills? (3) How realistic is it to expect general education teachers to accommodate and implement strategies for special needs students? It seems overly simplistic to assume that any single educational setting or teaching approach will be able to meet the needs of those students regardless of their abilities or disabilities (p. 20).

Implications for Music Education

In the past, music educators reported that they felt inadequate when dealing with special learners. Some of these inadequacies arose out of a lack of experience working with special needs students, a lack of support from school administration, and limited involvement in placement decisions. Quite possibly the feelings of inadequacy remain. This discussion is specifically concerned with the music educator's involvement in placement decisions regarding the inclusion of special needs students in the music classroom. How can one be proactive in this situation? Arguably, the most important thing one can do is not wait around for things to be done to you and your program. Affect placement decisions before they occur. Following are some ideas to consider.

Know What You Are Talking About

Typically, those in the profession are involved in their programs and are surprised when special needs students are placed in the music class. Many times the music educator feels put upon and blindsided. Are the guidance counselors and administrators free to place any special needs child in your class without your knowledge? Familiarize yourself with the law. Reread those paragraphs about mainstreaming in the Education for all Handicapped Children Act (P. L. 94-142). Research the regulations to Individuals with Disabilities Act (IDEA) and what it says about inclusion. These are readily available on the Internet (for example http:/ www.ed.gov/ offices/OSERS/IDEA).

Look to MENC for support. In *The School Music Program: Description and Standards* (MENC, 1986) it is stated that

> When handicapped students are mainstreamed into regular music classes:
> a. music educators are involved in placement decisions,
> b. placement is determined primarily on the basis of musical achievement,
> c. placement does not result in classes exceeding standard class size, and
> d. placement does not result in a disproportionate number of handicapped students in any class.

Do a little data collecting related to the number of special needs students you currently teach. Examine your class rosters and note how many special needs students are included in your classes compared to the overall number of students in your program (figure a percentage). Then compare that to the overall population of the school. You can get this information from the data clerk in your school if you do not know who is and who is not a special needs student. You might find out that you are already heavily implementing inclusion. Keep these numbers in mind when you ask for support later on.

Education of School Personnel

As the music teacher, you will need to let your needs be known to others in the school that make decisions affecting you and your program. This includes such personnel as the guidance counselor, administrative team, special education teachers, and case managers for the special needs students. You will find it beneficial to interact with these persons on a continuing basis throughout the year, not just during scheduling times. Invite these persons into your classroom to see what it is you do and that you are not babysitting and playing around. Make it plain that you are providing meaningful learning experiences to children. Point out that your curriculum requires students to use critical and creative thinking and is academic. Indicate that you welcome special needs students who can benefit from these learning experiences, however they should not be placed in music merely to comply with others' political agendas.

The law does not specify that 100 percent of all special needs students are to be placed in the music class in order to satisfy inclusion mandates. It is wise to continually return to the fact that the educational needs of the child are the most important factor and you as an educator are concerned for the placement that best meets the child's learning needs. Stress that you do not want to set the child up for failure and want to ensure maximum learning opportunities for all children.

Get in the Loop

Be proactive about placement by paying attention to the procedure. Make the effort to read the bulletin board that announces which students are being considered for inclusion and attend those meetings. Seek out the chairperson of the committee responsible for placement decisions and inquire about the placement procedures and meetings in your school.

Communicate with the special education teachers/guidance counselors. Set up formal meetings with these colleagues to discuss the student(s) being considered for inclusion in music. Do not accept an informal two-minute chat by the teacher's mailbox as a consultation. Offer to implement inclusion with the child on a trial basis (e.g., a month trial period) while holding off on putting it in the IEP document. Admittedly, these suggestions do take time away from your schedule, but the payoff is improved placement decisions affecting your program into which you have given your input.

Support Issues

Special needs students are afforded supports toward their educational endeavors. These can be in the form of materials, equipment, or personnel. Don't be shy about asking for those supports to accompany the child to your class. Present the data you collected in the first suggestion above related to educating yourself. For example, if the child needs music enlarged because of a sight problem, ask for that service to be provided. State that you will need to have someone enlarge or darken the music or you will need to be given access to equipment that will make the adaptation in order for this child's learning experience to be meaningful. It is best if support requirements can be stated when placement is initially being considered, however, they can be requested at any time.

A staff member can also give support in the form of assistance to the special learner. Ask for personnel to attend music class with the child if he/she needs assistance to stay on task, track music, or maintain appropriate behaviors that would make them successful in music. There are several types of teacher's aides available. Some are assigned to a particular special education classroom (teacher assistant to a self-contained class for learning disabled), some are assigned specifically to general education teachers to support inclusion (assistance-in-learning aide), some are assigned to a particular student all day (enhanced learning aide) and some are interpreters. Be assertive in asking for help. You might not get 100 percent assistance, but you may get some help. Start with the most severe cases requiring assistance and work backwards.

Use of a Rubric

When initially considering a child for inclusion in the music class, it would be helpful to provide the placement team with the following items to contemplate. These items are adapted from Coleman (1996, p. 153) and Gladfelter (1996, p. 195) and put into the following table format to provide a rubric. (See figure 1.)

Music educators have long included special needs students in their classrooms. Unfortunately, placements are not always appropriate. "Responsible inclusion requires careful planning and adequate support before any student with disabilities is placed in a regular class" (Wilson, p. 22). Music educators must take steps in advance to ward off improper placements and "dumping." It requires some time and effort on your part. Better placement results from better involvement in the procedure. Take the time and initiative to educate yourself and your staff, to become a part of the process, and to research resources that will yield improved learning situations for the special learner. Advocate for yourself and your program as well as the special needs child.

References

Adamek, M. S. (1996). In the beginning: A review of early special education services and legislative/regulatory activity affecting the teaching and placement of special learners. In B.L. Wilson, (Ed.), *Models of Music Therapy Interventions in School Settings: From Institution to Inclusion* (pp. 3–12). Silver Spring, MD: American Music Therapy Association, Inc.

Glatfelter, N. D. (1996). Music therapy for learners with learning disabilities in a private day school. In B. L. Wilson, (Ed.), *Models of Music Therapy Interventions in School Settings: From Institution to Inclusion* (pp. 184–199). Silver Spring, MD: American Music Therapy Association, Inc.

MENC. (1986). *The school music program: Description and standards*, 2nd ed. Reston, VA: MENC.

Snell, A. M. (1996). Music therapy for learners with autism in a public school setting. In B.L. Wilson, (Ed.), *Models of Music Therapy Interventions in School Settings: From Institution to Inclusion* (pp. 156–183). Silver Spring, MD: American Music Therapy Association, Inc.

Wilson, B. L. (1996). Changing times: The evolution of special education. In B.L. Wilson, (Ed.), *Models of Music Therapy Interventions in School Settings: From Institution to Inclusion* (pp. 13–26). Silver Spring, MD: American Music Therapy Association, Inc.

This article first appeared in the October 2000 issue of the Florida Music Director. *Reprinted by permission.*

Figure 1. Rubric for inclusion decisions in music class

	Independently	With a few verbal reminders	With adult support staff member
The student can stay seated for the duration of the class.			
The student can remain quiet at appropriate times during the class.			
The student can interact appropriately with peers.			
The student can keep to him/herself without distracting other students from learning.			
The student can keep his/her hands to him/herself and avoid hitting or other physical aggression.			
The student can respect musical equipment.			
The student can use classroom materials in an appropriate manner.			
The student can actively participate in at least one of the classroom activities with/without modification.			
The student can follow directions.			
The student can work independently.			
The student can accept praise/encouragement.			
The student can have a meaningful musical experience.			

Question 1. Will material support be available to enable adaptations to musical instruction and materials? O Yes O No

Question 2. Will there be an adult support staff member available to attend the class with the child at the scheduled time? O Yes O No

Inclusion Strategies that Work

Alice M. Hammel

When PL 94-142, now named IDEA, was passed, music teachers and administrators began preparing to include special learners in their classrooms. More than twenty-five years after the implementation of IDEA, we are still learning how to include special learners in our classrooms!

Through research and study, some important strategies have been identified. These strategies have been used in many music classrooms with great success.

Know Your Students

Music teachers who plan ahead for inclusion may find the process much easier. One suggestion is to talk to your school guidance counselor or administrator about students on your class roll. Check with classroom teachers of these students and be aware of any special services these students may receive in their general classroom. Also, if possible, get IEP (Individualized Education Program) summaries (may also be called student profiles or adaptations/modifications sheets) on all special learners in your classes, and review behavior management plans, curricular adaptation suggestions, and whether the student participates alone or with a "shadow" or aide.

If a student participates in a special education class, ask a special education staff member to review with you various limiting conditions associated with each student who has an IEP. They will gladly help you understand the "alphabet soup" of special education and will be up-to-date on any changes. Identify "strong" students who will possibly be good "friends" for a special student who may need help. The school guidance counselor may be able to help identify students. If possible, contact some students before school begins through postcards, emails, phone calls, or other forms of communication to "welcome" them to your class.

Know Your Special Education Faculty

Take the time to get to know the special education faculty at your school. Visit their classrooms and let them know that you are ready and willing to teach their students. This will help if any "problems" occur later. Know which special education teacher is primarily responsible for each special learner in your class. One teacher will be responsible for seeing that the Individualized Education Program (IEP) goals are met. This person is sometimes referred to as the case manager. Know the "specialties" of each special education teacher. Some are adept at brainstorming behavior modifications, others are better at curriculum adaptations. The school guidance counselor, administrator, or the teachers themselves will be good sources of information.

Invite the special education teachers to visit your classroom and offer any advice regarding the physical set-up of the room. Ask about possible modifications to your classroom procedures as well. They can be a wealth of information. Develop a good working relationship with these teachers. Let them know that you value the inclusion of their students in your classroom.

Know Your Special Education Staff Members

Get to know any special education paraprofessionals. If a student has an aide in the general classroom, that aide may also be in the music classroom with the student. Ask questions about specific situations or students. The shadows or aides are with the students all day. They may have some ideas about how specific students learn best. Invite the paraprofessionals to observe your class if they are not going to be a part of each class time. Allow them to offer suggestions based on their experiences.

Know Your Administration

Get to know your administration before the school year starts. Develop a positive working relationship with them and let them know how willing you are to teach all students in the school.

Ask about the possibility of attending an IEP meeting for a student in your class. Let them know that you consider this an important part of preparation to teach special learners. Know the procedures used by your administration regarding behavior and general noncompliance by students in classrooms. Determine whether any of the students in your class are under a different set of "rules" regarding behavior. Your knowledge of current laws and practice will help here.

Know How to Advocate for the 'Least Restrictive Environment'

"Least restrictive environment" is one of the most discussed sections of special education law. Students are to participate with their classmates in the "least restrictive environment." This means that they should be placed in classes where they will be successful with the least amount of modifications and adaptations. This does not mean that all your music classes are necessarily the "least restrictive environment" for all students. If a student is receiving all the modifications and adaptations you can provide and is still not successful in your class, another placement may actually be the "least restrictive environment" for that student. Students included in the general classroom setting for academic classes may or may not be included in other classes. Least restrictive environment is not universal.

In general, be prepared to teach all students, but be cognizant that not all students will succeed in your class. When you have tried all available modifications, consulted with special education faculty and staff, met with administrators, and followed suggestions by all of the faculty and staff, the student may still not be ready to succeed in your classroom. If nothing has helped, you have the right to suggest that the student be removed from your classroom. This is a last resort measure; however, it is within your realm to ask that the IEP be amended, the student be removed, an aide be present, or any other modification you deem necessary for the success of that student and other students in the class.

Know your instructional methods and materials and how to adapt them for special learners

There are many ways to adapt methods and materials for special learners. Not all adaptations will work for all students; however, if you continue to try new techniques, you are more likely to be successful.

- Use an overhead projector or computer enhanced image to enlarge materials (music, books, sheet music) as much as possible and provide written materials for all spoken instruction. A "picture" schedule is good for nonreaders and students with autism. Polaroid photographs of information also work well.
- Allow students a hands-on examination of all new materials, equipment, and instruments during introduction of a concept. This kinesthetic approach combined with the visual and aural instructional elements will help students learn according to their modality.
- Allow students to tape record rehearsals or lectures and to record a test or assignment. Allow students to respond to tests or assignments on the tape, orally, or in writing.
- Provide music or reading materials in advance to allow time for arrangements to be made for special learners.
- Use Velcro strips to help students hold mallets or small instruments. Sticks can also be wrapped with tape or foam rubber to facilitate handling.
- Jingle bells or cymbals can be sewn onto a band or ribbon and tied to the wrist. Straps and cords can be used to attach rhythm instruments to wheelchairs or walkers for students who may drop them during class.
- Code music or instruments with colors or symbols to help students remember notes or rhythms. A highlighter or colored pens/chalk can be used to help a student focus on a specific part of the music or book.
- A felt board or other raised texture board can be used with heavy rope to demonstrate the concept of a staff to students who learn kinesthetically or are visually impaired.
- Provide a written rehearsal schedule for students to follow. These can be on the chalk or bulletin board or placed in folders.
- Individualize some assignments for students who may not be able to complete the quantity of homework other students can. Check the IEP to make sure you are following the modifications listed.
- Make use of computers for students who need extra drill and practice.
- Separate rhythmic and melodic assignments until special learners can combine the two.
- Limit the use of words not yet in the student's vocabulary and be consistent with the terminology you do use.
- Allow students to help plan their own instructional accommodations and be a partner in the process.
- When preparing music for use by special learners, several adaptations can be made. The teacher can indicate tempo and meter, mark the student's part, allow students to highlight music, Write measure numbers and breath marks in the student's part, create visual aids for difficult words, and provide visual cues for score markings and phrase lengths.
- When using written assessments with special learners, provide accurate and complete study guides. Help focus study efforts on important events, ideas, and vocabulary. Use this tool to help students organize and sequence information.
- Use short tests at frequent intervals to encourage students to work at an even pace rather than postponing the study of a large amount of material until just before a long exam. This also provides a student some room to perform poorly on a single test without significantly compromising the grade for the entire marking period.
- Allow students to use a word bank. They may remember concepts, but have difficulty recalling spelling.
- Vary the style of test items used. Using a variety of test items will prevent a student from being

unduly penalized for having difficulty with a particular type of question.

- Place a rubber strip on the back of a ruler or use a magnetic ruler to help students measure or draw lines without slipping. Use adhesive-backed Velcro to attach items to a desk or wheelchair lap tray.
- Allow students to use pens (felt tip) or pencils (soft lead) that require less pressure or use a computer to complete assessments or assignments.
- Wait to prompt students for verbal answers to questions after at least 5 seconds have passed. They may need a longer period of time to process the question and determine an appropriate response. It may help to "call on" the student only when his/her hand is raised. This may lower any possible frustration level and prevent student embarrassment.
- If an accommodation or modification is listed in the IEP, all teachers must follow it.

Know the physical arrangement of your classroom and how to adapt it for special learners

A teacher who runs a well-organized and tidy classroom will help special learners be successful. It is important for teachers to orient special learners to the classroom and make them aware of safety issues. If you make any physical changes to the room, inform the special learners in advance, if possible. This applies to all special learners as a change in routine can be very difficult for them.

Teachers can make special physical arrangements for special learners with low or no vision. Reserve front seats for these students and make sure they are not near windows or uncontrolled lighting to prevent glare or other light issues. Students with physical disabilities should be integrated into the physical set-up of your classroom. These students will appreciate being in the middle of the classroom action even though integration of their wheelchairs, walkers, or other equipment may initially require some extra effort.

In general, when you make a change to the routine, mark the changes in several ways in the classroom (on the board, near folders, or equipment used for class). Keep the classroom neat and clear of clutter, if possible, and seat special learners near equipment if students are going to be moving to that equipment during class.

Know your classroom management style and how to adapt It for special learners

Classroom management can be one of the most frustrating aspects of teaching special learners. Some students are educated according to a different set of expectations, especially if their behavior is a part of their identified disability. Music teachers who are aware of the students who are in this category will be able to be more consistent and will not run the risk of applying a disciplinary procedure that will be overturned by the administration.

Some general classroom management ideas are universal for all students. One important strategy that music teachers use every day is to use seating arrangements to facilitate good behavior management. Teachers who provide a rehearsal outline for students who can read may be able to increase the amount of time a student is on-task. Many teachers use a prearranged signal or word to notify the student when his/her behavior is not appropriate. This gives the student an opportunity to modify behavior before other students in the class are aware of it. In general, work with special education teachers. Try to use the same behavior management plan used in the general or special education classroom to provide greater consistency for the special learner. Try to be available for parent/teacher conferences, particularly for students who are having difficulty in your class. If possible, ask to be included in the conference held with the parents to let parents know about the difficulty a student is having in your music classroom.

Some well known, and highly successful techniques are to:

- Make sure all students know they are of value to the group.
- Be flexible and modify classroom expectations when necessary to help all students succeed in your classroom.
- Avoid power struggles with students. Provide specific instructions and feedback regarding behavior privately rather than risk a verbal struggle in front of the class.
- Be positive whenever possible (80%–20% is ideal). Be sure you know what reinforces a behavior (this can vary according to the student).

Know How and When to Ask for Help

Before asking for outside help, make sure you have done everything possible to solve the situation yourself. If you have already tried several solutions, you will be better able to precisely define the problem. When you do ask for help, begin by asking the instructional aide, classroom teacher, or special education teacher. They will be able to describe their strategies and give you some ideas. If these strategies do not work, request a conference with the parents (or guardians), teachers, and student, if practical. Try to create a new plan. Make sure the plan has a definite beginning and ending date, and make a date to meet again if the plan is not working.

If all efforts continue to fail, ask for help from the administration. At this point, you will have gathered a lot of information and will be able to show that you have sought the advice and help of the teachers and parents (or guardians) of the student. If nothing seems to work, all personnel are involved, all accommodations are being made, and the student is still failing to succeed in the class, then your classroom may not be the "least restrictive environment" for that student. You do have the right to request that the student be removed from your classroom. You will have shown at this point that you have done everything possible to insure success. This is your right.

There are many sources of help available to you. The instructional aides, classroom teachers, special education teachers, site administration, central administration, and local agencies are all there to help you. Seek outside help whenever necessary to secure the best possible classroom environment for all students. A listing of agencies and contact persons are listed on my Web site: www.hammel.us under the heading of "special learners."

Many special learners have low self-esteem and are easily frustrated. Celebrating each small success helps build student/teacher relationships and reminds students of their value to you and the school community. You can be a positive influence that a student will remember forever. I encourage you to seek outside help whenever necessary to secure the best possible classroom environment for all special learners. I also encourage you to embrace these very special young people. Your willingness to actively include special learners in your music classrooms will be greatly appreciated by your students and treasured by the parents who trust you with the music education of their most precious possessions: their children.

This article first appeared in the Winter 2002 issue of the Massachusetts Music News. *Reprinted by permission.*

Soothing Sounds: How to Use Music with Special Learners

Arthur Harvey

Music has far greater power to affect our minds and bodies than most individuals realize. I was aware even as a young child how much music affected my own energy level, mood, and thinking. At age nine when I was playing the organ for a worship service, I began to notice the power I had as a musician. One Sunday, it dawned on me that the way I played the music had an effect on others; I could control the way the offering was received by changing the speed of the piece of music. So, I gradually increased the tempo, and to my delight the men moved faster. Then, I slowed down the tempo, and the ushers walked slower.

At that moment, I experientially understood a phenomenon in music that is an underlying principle for much music therapy activity and for educational and personal uses of music in our lives. Music can affect us physiologically and psychologically through a process called "entrainment." As music is listened to, and if we "resonate" with it, it can change us. Depending on how certain musical elements are combined, music can excite or calm, stimulate or relax, and control or free us or others.

Music has a calming effect. When our then 5-year-old daughter Cathy was having difficulty going to sleep, we found that playing a recording of Beethoven's Pastoral Symphony (No. 6) was sufficiently calming to put her to sleep. I arrived at a hospital in Berea, Kentucky one day to conduct a therapeutic session in the extended care wing and found a 17-year-old male crying. I was told he had been crying for over two days, and everyone was on edge. The staff asked if I could do anything with music to calm him. I began playing music that mirrored his agitated mood (loud, dissonant, disorganized, complex) and gradually changed the music to reflect the transition toward becoming calm (softer, consonant, ordered, simple). Within 20 minutes he had stopped crying and went to sleep. The nurses called me a "miracle worker." Music has that marvelous, God-given power to "calm the savage beast," as the Bible describes David's music calming King Saul.

In special education classes, I have used music for both therapeutic and educational purposes. Because music affects many levels of our brains, it is uniquely able to affect emotions and set the mood of the classroom or home. Music can be used in conjunction with almost any activity throughout the day, with any person, no matter what his or her disability may be, no matter what the age. Following are some ways that music can be used in the lives of those learners with special needs, with suggestions of the type of music to be most effective in a particular area.

Use music:

1. To awaken an individual (in the morning or from a nap). Start with gentle music, softly played, and gradually increase tempo and volume.
2. To increase energy. Increase volume as well as tempo (from 60–70 beats per minute to 90–120 beats per minute).
3. For exercising. A steady, strong beat increases endurance and helps motivate and organize steady movements during muscle development time. It can also be a diversion, as well as a pain-reduction mechanism.
4. During eating. Quiet, moderate to slow tempo music can aid digestion and help keep individuals calmer and quieter.
5. During bathroom breaks. Calming music can be a good diversion and helps relax muscles.
6. To set the mood in the room. The kind of music chosen can set the mood as learners enter the room. If they need to be energized, lively music awakens energy and expectations. If they need to be calmed, gradually decreasing volume and tempo can calm them down.
7. To welcome class members. Singing greetings and names has more impact than just speaking the names.
8. To teach information, ideas, and concepts. Information learned through singing activates both hemispheres of the brain and increases memory function.
9. To give directions. Singing instructions is often more effective than saying them.
10. To help create an environment for reading. Play soft, instrumental music while students read. It helps diminish distractions and keeps their minds from wandering.
11. To time assignments. Let the playing of a musical selection be the timing activity rather than the clock.
12. For motor development. Many musical activities can increase motor skills development. Many percussion instruments provide immediate feedback while developing motor skills.
13. For release of emotions/feelings. Playing aggressively on a drum or other percussion instrument provides a safe vehicle for the release of strong feelings.
14. As an alternative communication system. Playing question and answer games with instruments provides another communication opportunity for members with limited verbal development.
15. For social skill development. Learning to take turns, to be a leader, and to share is more easily facilitated in a musical situation.
16. For rewards. Use listening time or playing time as a contingency for completion of a task or appropriate behavior.
17. As a recreation or leisure activity. The rich variety of musical resources available today makes it possible for almost anyone to be successful in music making for pure pleasure or joy.
18. For going to sleep. Quiet, slow, calm music is wonderful for a transition from being awake to being asleep. Because music can alter consciousness so easily, it is a natural to provide a secure environment for peaceful sleep.

Music Activities

Music activities used in special education include: moving to/with music; playing instruments or creating sounds on objects that serve as instrument substitutes; singing; listening to music; creating music/sounds or words and movements to music; learning information about music, instruments, composers, or learning to read music.

Certain instruments lend themselves well to the adaptability needed with persons who have special needs. A variety of percussion/rhythm instruments is a basic starting place. Kazoos are great for musical as well as speech and respiratory development. Recorders, ukuleles, omnichords, chime bells, and adaptive guitars are also used successfully with special members.

Teachers need to take advantage of the variety of recordings that are available today through companies like Kimbo and Educational Activities. As I concluded the original version of this article published in *Special Education Today* April/May/ June 1996, "May God continue to use the special gift of music to enrich the lives of those special individuals He has entrusted to us to teach and love."

This article first appeared in the April 2000 issue of Hawaii's HMEA Bulletin. *Reprinted by permission.*

Music for All: Focus on Autism

Carol Howell

Greetings! I hope your year has been successful so far. I thought I'd take the opportunity in this column to share with you some activity ideas for special learners—this month focusing on children with autism. This year, I seem to have a great abundance of young children with autism or children with autistic tendencies. According to Lois Birkenshaw-Fleming, in her book *Music For All*, these tendencies include withdrawn behavior, severe language dysfunction, perseveration, a desire for order, and sensitivity to sound. Here are some favorite activities:

Awareness of Self

Body part identification songs. I try to use a number of songs with the body parts actually named in the song:

"Put Your Hands Up in the Air," *Learning Basic Skills*, Vol. I (Hap Palmer)

"Put Your Finger in the Air," *Music and You*, Grade K (Greg and Steve also have a jazzy version.)

"Clap Your Hands," *Music and You*, Grade 1

"Hokey Pokey"

"Bean Bag Rock," *Bean Bag Coordination Activities* (Kimbo)

"It's a Small World," stick dance, *Lumni Stick Activities in Early Childhood* (Kimbo)

Awareness of Others

Hello song with name. Children choose who to sing to next.

Hello, (name), how do you do,
1 1 1 1 2 2 1

How do you do, how do you do.
7 2 2 1 7 3 2 1

Hello, (name), how do you do,
1 1 1 1 2 2 1

How do you do today.
7 2 2 1 2 1

Instrument pass

(Name)'s gonna play the drum,
5 5 6 5 1 1 3

Play the drum, play the drum,
1 1 7-6 1 1 3

And then (he'll/she'll) pass it on.
1 3 3 2 2 1

"Bean Bag Pass," *Bean Bag Coordination Activities* (Kimbo)

Instrument imitation. I use a big bass drum turned on its side. At first, I echo the child and then gradually work towards them echoing me either rhythmically, dynamically, or by tempo.

Sound songs are a good way of facilitating verbal expression. Songs, such as "I Took a Trip to Grandmother's Farm" (Hap Palmer), "Have You Seen My Cow" (Ella Jenkins), "Mi Chacra" (My Farm), with animal sounds and environment sounds are great. It's really interesting to see what these kids link onto. I have one student who is very withdrawn, but one day as we were doing a train song, he suddenly came alive. It turns out that he has a real fascination with cars, trains, and trucks. Since that time I've included a car, train, or truck song in the lesson and he's now starting to gradually participate in other songs. It is said that often autistic children will develop relationships with objects before people.

Also, many autistic children have a sensitivity to higher frequencies. Turning down the treble on the stereo, or using low pitched instruments helps.

This article first appeared in the November/December 1997 issue of the Maryland Music Educator. *Reprinted by permission.*

Inclusion, Not Intrusion

Betty Krebs

You've just gotten word that two new students, who happen to have disabilities, will be joining your music class later this week. Your school district policy is one of inclusion. The students will be instructed in regular classrooms with students of like chronological age during the entire school day. Panic time! You weren't prepared for this in your undergraduate classes. You are already too busy meeting the national, state, and local standards in your large music classes, not to mention preparing for impending mandated performances. What will you do now? What will the new students be able to do, and how will you be able to accommodate their needs?

Even though you believe you are, you're not alone. Begin by looking for a special education facilitator in your building or district. Don't worry about the title. The person's title changes from school to school and by district, but there is a person who is hired to assist you in your planning and your preparation of class materials for your special education students. Get to know this special education facilitator and establish a good working relationship. It is worth your time and effort. Set up a meeting with this person as soon as possible. Bring along some ideas of things you think might work well, along with some questions that you have about what to expect from the new students.

In the meantime, check the student records for a current IEP (Individualized Education Program). Federal and state law requires a current IEP for each special education student. In the IEP, you will find information about past participation and student progress.

There will be goals and objectives for this year, along with a time frame in which to accomplish these. There will be lists of courses and activities. Finally, there will be additional information about the student and a listing of needed services. Note the disability classification of the student.

Sometimes an IEP is revealing in what it does not say. Do you see evidence of past experiences in music? Is music listed in the planned curriculum or as an avenue in achieving any of the goals in the IEP? Think of ways in which this newly gleaned information will assist you in making accommodations in your regular music classes so that all of your students will be able to participate at the highest level possible.

Use a variety of avenues in planning adaptations. For example, some students who happen to have difficulty in hearing or attending to the lesson need preferential seating in order to see demonstrations. The teacher and classmates need to add visual cues in order to increase understanding. Students who happen to have difficulty in moving may need to be assigned to adapted or alternative activities. Perhaps adding a computer, a tape of the lesson either before or after class, enlarged copies, simplified handouts, making a simple study guide, or carrying out a behavior plan established by someone else will be just the accommodations needed.

Consider strength and interest areas of the students. You may find a functioning level well above what you expected. It is possible that you will need to make no adaptations at all. On the other hand, don't be surprised to find splinter skills in the students, such as excellence in pitch, but poor rhythm, etc. Can the student move to the music, sing, play an instrument, listen intently to the music, read, write, or create music? You will find areas that you will be able to utilize. At what level does the student participate? Will the student be able to show an awareness of what is happening musically, imitate a leader, initiate a musical response, or perhaps evaluate someone else's response? Will the student be able to complete tasks independently, with verbal cues, with gestural prompts, or is physical help needed? Will the student need a buddy to assist or is an adult helper, such as an instructional aide, needed?

Some teachers have difficulty in evaluating, planning for, and including students who appear to function at the severe/profound level. Look for simple skills that can be capitalized upon or strengthened. Are the students able to make eye contact with a leader, attend to the lesson material for an increasing length of time? Do the students recognize faces, instruments, or music. Do you see reaction to phrase endings by a simple movement of the body, a blink of the eye, or even a change in the breathing pattern?

Perhaps the students are able to communicate by using simple gestures, facial expressions, and other means to give simple answers such as "done," "more," "yes," "no," "hello," and "goodbye." Can the student follow a one-step command? Using very simple language, ask a student to do just one simple, short thing. Is the student able to participate while using a pressure switch, a computer, or some type of adaptive device? Can students make choices between two or among several? Can they match and sort?

Thinking of an even more basic level of skills, do the students remain seated, refrain from making inappropriate noises, use materials appropriately, participate in at least one activity, appear to gain meaning from the class? These skills need to be worked on if not already present. Offer a positive musical activity that can only be done without the unwanted behavior.

By virtue of your job as a music teacher, you are quite experienced in working with a variety of students at varying levels of functioning. If at all possible, use a strength area in the first session. Plan at least one activity during this (and every) class in which the student will be able to participate. Don't be surprised if you get little or a delayed response at first. It takes time to adjust to a new setting. Consider the rest of the class. Will other students benefit from this activity as well? If not, how can you change it so some will? If an adult helper (such as an instructional aide) is needed, do you have time to prepare the adaptation for the session in mind? If not, change or delay it, or ask the facilitator to assist.

Now that you have considered a number of avenues and a variety of accommodations, you are ready to pick the appropriate ones (your nominations for the best practice) and fit them into your class lesson plans. Stick the rest of them into your back pocket for another day. Everyone will benefit from your thoughtful planning!

This article first appeared in the Spring 1999 issue of the Illinois Music Educator. *Reprinted by permission.*

Success in Savanna: It Takes a Community to Include Special Learners in High School Band

Christine Lapka

By all accounts, Savanna High School (Northwest Illinois) has successfully included special education students in its high school band. Because high school educators are asked to deal with the largest achievement discrepancy (ability levels that are much lower than the chronological age of a student), it merits repetition. Savanna High School's inclusion of special education students goes far beyond a person simply sitting in an ensemble. The students are as essential as the chime part in "The Liberty Bell March."

Given the frequency of requests for information on how to include special learners in performing groups, this story is exciting. So you ask, what makes it work? To investigate, I traveled to Savanna to observe and interview the teachers. I found the inclusion of an entire self-contained special education class. As the title implies, more than one person is involved in making this integration a true music education. In addition, a unified philosophy and specific teaching techniques help to round out the elements of this integrated program.

Collaboration is key in successful inclusive programs (Friend & Bursuck, 1999). Likewise, the Illinois State Board of Education (2002) recognizes the importance of collaboration by making it part of the Illinois Professional Teaching Standards for All Teachers. In Savanna, music teacher Mark Bressler, special education teacher Renee Simmons, all band members, and parents work together to insure the success of the program.

Renee is present in all band rehearsals and is given Mark's rehearsal plan in advance. Discussion takes place the day before or immediately prior to Renee's involvement in the rehearsal. In fact, at the last minute (very last minute—during the concert when she could not decline) she was asked to direct a piece. Even though this was part of a humorous prank, it is a step towards seeing the special education teacher in the music instructor role. By her own admission, Renee is not knowledgeable about music and relies on Mark to be the curriculum specialist. She sees herself as the delivery expert and is fascinated with "the puzzle or mystery" of modifications. In addition, Mark and Renee have a deep respect for each other. They are in tune with the give and take of the collaborative process: "Team teaching is like a good marriage" (Simmons, 2003).

The students in this ensemble mirror the respect of their teachers. Because of the number of inexperienced members in the percussion section, the section leader and experienced members act as extraordinary peer mentors. They spend all available time guiding and assisting their team. Likewise, the entire group seems willing to work together. When Mark models a better tambourine grip, all other students are patient and begin discussing their own parts. At one point in the rehearsal, the director mentioned an intonation problem with a borrowed flute. When the group stopped playing, the two neighboring players nearly dove into their cases to produce tuning/cleaning rods to solve the problem. I suspect that students are responding to the teacher and percussion section models because all of the members collaborated when the band stopped playing.

Parents make up the last collaborative component. When the marching band performs or the band travels, parents are available to assist as needed. Renee corresponds with her parents on a daily or near daily basis. In addition to assisting during trips and performances, Mark is thankful for the parents' words of encouragement for his inclusive efforts. This teaching team shares a common philosophy of focusing on a person's strengths. When needed, the teachers assist students by promoting "abilities and not disabilities." Renee reports her fear of having the students participate in contest and evening performances when medications are less effective at controlling behaviors. Mark firmly believes that the students are valuable members of the group. Their abilities contribute to the performance and he hopes that distracting behaviors will be ignored or lessen with experience. This philosophy paid off when the band received a first place sight-reading score at IHSA organizational contest. When discussing the total inclusion of the students, Renee stated, "Mark is not as interested in external competition—he is more interested in internal competition." When he pushes the students to do their best, the results take care of themselves.

Peer tutoring is a recommended method for the integration of students (Friend & Bursuck, 1999). During the observation of the band, I was inspired by the student's total engagement in making better music. Earlier, I addressed the amount of peer collaboration during the rehearsal. It was remarkable. I expected them to stop and talk about their social lives but they showed their neighbors a trill fingering or alternate trombone position. I heard one young person say, "maybe you need to write in the natural you keep missing." Beyond watching the collaborative teacher models, students are encouraged to help new members (special education students). It appears that tutor roles have proliferated through the entire ensemble. The method used for special education students has had a positive effect on the entire group.

Other modifications were used for individual students. A few students with visual perception problems were assisted by color coding notes. In many cases, color coding could be stopped after a given period of time. Modeling and rote teaching techniques were effective for some students. Others required aural and visual cues to perform. In all cases, adaptations were selected with the student's needs in mind.

The current program did not happen overnight. "It morphed into what it is today" (Simmons, 2003). Aided by preferred teaching strategies and a common inclusive philosophy, the program took its first steps. Mark was assisted by the alliance of involved persons. It takes a community of learners, teachers, and parents to make diversity work. Congratulations Savanna!

References

Friend, M., & Bursuck, W. (1999). *Including Students with Special Needs: A Practical Guide for Classroom Teachers* (2nd ed.). (Short, R., & Reilly, A., Eds.). Needham Heights, MA: Allyn and Bacon.

Illinois State Board of Education. (2002). Professional Teaching Standards for All Teachers. Division of Professional Preparation and Recruitment. Available: www.isbe.net/profprep

Mark Bressler. March 11, 2003. personal communication.

Renee Simmons. March 11, 2003. personal communication.

This article first appeared in the Spring 2003 issue of the Illinois Music Educator. *Reprinted by permission.*

You Need a Therapist

Christine Lapka

While sitting in the back yard of my home, I looked up to see a pair of masked eyes peering down from the chimney. I immediately realized that I needed professional help! After several telephone calls to friends and the animal shelter, I was referred to a chimney sweep for his help to remove the family of raccoons. His advice was easy to follow and worked like a charm. In fact, in just one short hour the baby raccoon was quite anxious. The event drew a small crowd of people to my house at a busy intersection. After a good deal of squealing (by the baby) and explanations to worried neighbors (by me), the mother raccoon returned to prepare for the big move.

Is the remedy making you curious? Music! Music was the prescription. The trick was a radio in the fireplace for a period of 24 hours (tune to your least favorite station for added adversity). My friends and neighbors thought this was an appropriate solution for a music educator.

The reaction led me to a question posed by a public school colleague who called wanting information about a particular study regarding music, reading comprehension, and learning disabled students. She wanted to know what I knew about the study and my views on incorporating it in music classes. We agreed the information was interesting and further discussed possible incorporation in a general music classroom. However, the reading teachers in the school actually wanted the music teacher to use music as remedial treatment for low reading comprehension. Therefore, I looked into studies related to music for nonmusical goals. Subsequent discussion here will provide brief descriptions of studies involving therapeutic uses of music with disabled children. The purpose of the dialogue is to keep music educators informed of related research. However, the content of the studies raises the question, "is this applicable to music education?"

LaBach's (1959) study looked at the influence of background music on reading comprehension. A standardized reading test was administered while students listened to a tape of relaxing orchestral music. The music did not significantly affect test scores. After looking at his research design, LaBach found the one time use of background music a possible inadequacy. The single dose of music during a testing situation may not have been enough to cause improved reading comprehension. It seems a bit simple to suggest that instant improvements in understanding occur after selecting music and flipping a switch. In the epilogue, he wondered if a prolonged treatment plan would yield different effects.

Using LaBach's research as a springboard, Helfrich (1973) decided to use slow and fast rock music over a prolonged period as the basis of his investigation. He chose rock music because students in LaBach's study had favorable attitudes toward music and specifically asked for fast popular music. Helfrich takes his investigation a step further by deciding to target only disabled readers, performing below grade level one year or more. Three treatment groups were established. All groups received remedial instruction by a certified reading specialist using materials developed for disabled readers. Group 1 was given instruction without background music. Groups 2 and 3 listened to slow (70 ± 3) and fast (126 ± 6) instrumental rock music respectively. In addition, students were seated to provide a constant 70-decibel level of sound.

Even with the extended 12-week treatment, rock music did not improve reading test scores. Still, its use did not hinder normal progress. In addition, questionnaires indicate students prefer the use of music in instruction. Helfrich believes the importance of music might have a psychological effect suitable for further study.

A more recent study seems to surface in discussions involving learning disabled (LD) students. Wiley-Khaaliq (1990) used piano music by Sergei Rachmaninoff as background music during four testing sessions. Two groups were used for the investigation. Each group of LD students completed two forms of the test. First without background music and next with music controlled for a decibel range of 60–65. In this case, the differences between the music and nonmusic tests were significant. On the average, tests given during the quiet romantic piano music yielded greater comprehension. Yet, five of the thirty subjects did not improve during the background music situation. Although background music can facilitate reading comprehension, individual variation should be expected.

Wiley-Khaaliq attributes the success of the background music to the selection of music with slow tempos. She bases her idea on research of tempos related to the human heart at rest by Lozanov (1978). He believes a tempo of sixty beats a minute reduces the heart rate and blood pressure and subsequently causes an anxiety-free state. However fascinating his research is, without comparing faster music in the Wiley-Khaaliq study, we cannot assume the tempo of the music caused the improvement in comprehension. Because earlier studies used orchestral music, timbre could play a part in learning outcomes. Replicating the study with tempo or tone color controls could yield results that are more conclusive.

Background music was also the subject of investigation in a 1996 study to determine its effect on behavior (Campbell). The study found soft background music compared to no music reduces out-of-seat and talk-out behaviors. When comparing soft music to moderate music, both improved targeted behaviors with soft music having a greater impact. In like manner, soft music enhanced on-task behavior of students and improved classroom performance.

After creating lessons and music activities focused on development of communication, the program was launched in an early childhood special education classroom (Frick, 2000). Subjects included students with communication delays, motor characteristics associated with cerebral palsy, severe developmental delays, and autistic-like behavior. During ten weeks of intense music use by the teacher and students, music increased vocalizations and created a social context for child interaction.

The previous studies use music to enhance or facilitate learning, but are they music education? Playing music for the raccoon in the fireplace was not music education. Similarly, music educators do not teach by simply including music during instruction. Unfortunately, some are troubled or confused when schools request their classes to cover areas outside of the music curriculum (excluding reciprocal curriculum integration). Music educators are not trained to teach other subject areas and are often hindered by limited contact time. Likewise, Hoffer (1993) suggests caution when music educators defend school music programs with extramusical reasons for existence.

A quandary is created when music specialists are expected to ready students for Illinois State Learning Outcomes and use precious music time to implement nonmusic programs in areas outside of a specialist's range of training. To solve the problem we need to look beyond the current "go ask the music teacher" mentality. When faced with the raccoon problem, I searched for the proper practitioner. As a profession, we need to extend a professional courtesy to the field of music therapy.

Music educators should suggest the services of music therapists when asked to use music for outcomes other than those found in the music curriculum. Music therapists are interested in school setting employment (Smith & Hariston, 1999). In a 1979 journal article, Alley calls for collaboration between music education and music therapy. Darrow (1996) feels the goals and objectives of music therapy and music education overlap and can be worked on simultaneously by both educators and therapists. MENC's Music Code of Ethics protects the domain of professional musicians (1986). Perhaps it is time to direct our attention to the domain of music therapy by insisting on the services of music therapists. In such cases, I do not believe therapists will jeopardize music education. I do believe their employment can ease some of the burden and confusion regarding the role of music education. When asked to use music classes as remedies for poor reading comprehension, music teachers can give professional advice by saying, "You need a therapist."

References

Alley, J. M. (1979). Music in the IEP: Therapy/education. *Journal of Music Therapy*, 16 (3). 111–127.

Campbell, D. (1996). *The effects of soft background music on compliance in the classroom: A case study of some New York City special education classrooms.* Dissertation Abstracts International, 57(06) 2432A. (University Microfilms No. ADG963356)

Darrow,. A. A. (1996). Research on mainstreaming: Implications for music therapists, in B. L. Wilson (Ed.), *Models of music therapy interventions in school settings: From institution to inclusion.* Silver Spring, MD: National Association for Music Therapy.

Frick, I. W. (2000). *A qualitative study of music and communication in musically rich early childhood special education classroom.* Dissertation Abstracts International, 60(08) 2868A. (University Microfilms No. ADG9940757)

Helfrich, D. C. (1973). The effect of rock music, controlled for tempo and volume, on disabled readers in remedial reading classes. (Doctoral dissertation. University of Georgia, 1972). Dissertation Abstracts International. 34 (06) 3024A.

Hoffer, C. R. (1993). *Introduction to music education* (2nd ed.). Belmont, California: Wadsworth Publishing.

LaBach, J. P. (1959) The effects of background music on reading comprehension and their relationship to various other characteristics in sixth grade students. (Doctoral dissertation, Syracuse University, 1959). Dissertation Abstracts International, 21 (02) 0350.

Lozanoy, G. (1978). Suggestology (in Bulgarian). Sofia, Bulgaria: Izdatelsvo Nauka I Izkustvo, 1971. English.

MENC. (1986). *Guidelines for performances of school music groups: Expectations and limitations.* Reston, VA: Author.

Smith, D. S., & Hariston, M. J. (1999). Music therapy in school settings: Current practice. *Journal of Music Therapy.* 36(4). 274-292.

Wiley-Khaaliq, R. (1990). A study of the effects of background music on reading comprehension of learning disabled students. (Doctoral dissertation, Southern Illinois University at Carbondale, 1990). Dissertation Abstracts International. 52(01) 0123A.

This article first appeared in the Fall 2001 issue of the Illinois Music Educator. *Reprinted by permission.*

Advocating for Assistive Technology for Students with Disabilities in Your School

Kimberly McCord

Kolby is a second grader who began losing his eyesight a year ago. He is completely blind in one eye and can see light and dark in the other eye. Last year in music he played instruments, learned dances and movement, and used the computer to compose. All of those activities have become much more limited for him this year. While the other children learn to play borduns on Orff instruments, Kolby does body percussion. While the rest of the class delights at creating songs in the Music Ace Doodle Pad (http://www.harmonicvision.com/), Kolby sits next to one child and listens to what she creates on the computer. Kolby still sings and does movement and, of course, plays many instruments, but his experience is not the same as the other students in his class.

Children with disabilities benefit from music as much as nondisabled children. Unfortunately music teachers continue to struggle with ways to fully include children with disabilities in their classes and ensembles. Often we do this with very little input into the child's Individual Education Plan (IEP). We do our best to find ways to include everyone in music but it can still be challenging to make sure everyone gets an equal experience. Assistive technology is a powerful tool you can use to equalize musical experiences. If you have a computer in your classroom, you can integrate it with hardware and software to help students access the computer. Assistive technology also includes the use of electronic instruments that help to make music accessible to some children with disabilities.

In the past thirteen years there have been changes to the original law that mandated free, appropriate public education in the least restrictive environment for all children with disabilities who qualify under the requirements. The Individuals with Disabilities Education Act of 1990 (IDEA) was amended in 1997 to require school teams preparing Individual Education Programs (IEP) to consider using assistive technology in the plan.

Generally, the purpose of using assistive technology is to enhance access and independence in learning for persons with disabilities. Assistive technology is defined as "any item, piece of equipment, or product system, whether acquired commercially off the shelf, modified, or customized, that is used to increase, maintain, or improve functional capabilities of children with disabilities" (IDEA, 1997). The purpose of assistive technology may include the augmentation of an individual's strengths so that his or her abilities counterbalance the effects of any disabilities or the provision of an alternate mode of performing a task so that disabilities are compensated or bypassed entirely (Lewis, 1993). Assistive technology may also serve as a leveraging agent, allowing students with disabilities to experience greater academic success and independence (Bryant, Bryant, & Raskind, 1998; Bryant & Seay, 1998; Raskind & Higgins, 1998). Moreover, the use of assistive technology by students with disabilities offers greater learning opportunities, serving as a conduit to enhancing access to the general education curriculum (Smith & Jones, 1999) and computer-based music instruction (Gregory, 2002). Congress passed the Technology-Related Assistance for Individuals with Disabilities Act in 1988 (otherwise known as the "Tech Act"). This act mandated each state to provide consumer driven services, to disseminate information related to assistive technology, and to address removal of assistive technology barriers for individuals (Bryant & Bryant, 2003).

Categories of Assistive Technology

For the purposes of this article I an going to put assistive technology in four general categories that have specific relevance to music education. Within these categories I will also list hardware and software that I have found helpful for different types of disabilities. The categories I use are vision/reading aids, computer/musical instrument aids, communication aids, and seating/positioning aids.

Vision/Reading Aids in music include screen magnification software or equipment, text-to-speech product systems (e.g., Kurzweil 3000), products that convert screen text to braille, and products that convert MIDI output to braille music, software products such as Band-in-a-Box that highlight text and music notation as the song plays. These products primarily help blind and visually impaired students, but also might be used with nonreaders or children who have difficulty focusing on text or music notation.

The second category of assistive technology is computer/musical instrument aids. These include devices such as a wide variety of adaptive keyboards, pointing devices, and alternative MIDI instruments. Students with physical disabilities benefit the most from these devices, however, children with limited speech or with severe learning disabilities may also be helped. Some children with learning disabilities that are severe benefit from an alternative approach that eliminates the dysfunctioning mode of leaning (visual, aural, kinesthetic) and instead focuses on a better functioning mode of learning. A computer/MIDI station is a multisensory approach to learning and children can learn to tune out the mode that gives them the most problems. For example, children with visual processing learning problems can look away from the computer screen or in some types of software you can adapt the screen to not show distracting information like multiple windows or animations. Computer and musical aids include alternative MIDI controllers such as the Soundbeam (http://www.soundbeam.co.uk/). The Soundbeam is an ultrasonic beam that responds to movement with MIDI sounds. The Soundbeam is accessible to children with limited movement or it can respond to larger movements such as a wheel chair moving across a room. The Soundbeam does not need a computer to be used; it connects the ultrasonic beam sensors (about the size of a small microphone) to a small box. Soundbeam has proven to be very successful with severely disabled students who, over time, discover they are the source of the sound they hear. Children with physical disabilities have an easier time playing sounds on the Soundbeam than they do with many of the more traditional instruments. The ultrasonic beam can be adjusted to be very wide to accommodate large movement or very small to accommodate something as precise as the movement of an eyebrow. Soundbeam can be used with computer software to notate an improvisation or to play with previously recorded tracks in a sequencer or Band-in-a-Box.

Soundchair and Soundbed, produced by the makers of the Soundbeam, allow children with physical disabilities to feel the vibrations of the sound triggered by the ultrasonic beam while seated or in a prone position. The bed or chair vibrates with the sound, which enables students who are deaf and hearing-impaired to feel sounds.

Traditional keyboard synthesizers can often be challenging for children with disabilities to use. Coordination is required to play the instrument, but children with motor issues struggle with playing one note at a time. Percussion controllers make use of rubber pads that can be programmed to respond to playing with sticks or hands. The larger surfaces of the drum pads help students with motor and visual disabilities access MIDI programmed sounds more easily than playing the actual acoustic instruments. Students with physical disabilities, such as muscular dystrophy, can lightly tap the pads with fingertips and the sound produced can be programmed to sound very forceful if desired. Roland is one company that makes affordable percussion pads (http://www.rolandus.com/products/subcategory.asp?catid=5&subcatid=26). Communication aids include products and equipment designed to help students with speech, writing, and hearing difficulties. These devices include communication boards, note taking devices, hearing aids, FM amplification systems, and accompaniment software with visual cues such as Band-in-a-Box (BIAB).

BIAB is a software program that creates rhythm-section accompaniments for just about any style or genre of music. Students are able to decide what sounds, tempo, and styles they would like to use to accompany melodies. Melodies can be either entered into the software program or songs that come with the program can be accessed in the program. Band-in-a-Box has a number of helpful features for music teachers to use with children with disabilities. Lyrics to songs may be entered into the program and during playback of the song words are highlighted. The percussion view features pictures of a number of percussion instruments that can be played by clicking the mouse on the picture. Children with disabilities can play software instruments such as maracas in the program using an adaptive mouse. A student with cerebral palsy who could not possibly hold a cymbal or even a mallet secure enough to play it, could have an easier time leaning his or her body into a large switch encased in soft fabric to activate the crash cymbals in BIAB.

BIAB can benefit many types of students with disabilities by offering visual cues that coordinate with what they hear. Seeing words highlighted as they sing or notes highlighted as they play helps some children to keep track of where they are in the music.

Using a device that visually enlarges information on a computer screen is helpful towards including children who otherwise might get confused and lost during some activities. Look for software that has strong contrast between light and dark similar to games that come with the CD-ROM program Making Music (http://www.creatingmusic.com). Kolby is able to use some of the games in this program that guides students to listen for same and different and click on the correct answer by selecting lightly colored balls that glow as the cursor is moved across them.

Another category of assistive technology is seating and positioning aids. These devices provide people with disabilities better stability, posture, and support. They can also increase access to classroom materials such as adaptive seating, wheelchair modifications, and mounting devices to hold instruments. Companies like West Music advertise a selection of devices that can help make playing instruments more accessible for children with physical disabilities. Different types of brackets help mount instruments like triangles to wheelchairs that enable children to better access instruments.

Resources for Learning More about Assistive Technology

Cost of assistive devices should not be a factor when designing education in the least restrictive environment. If students need these devices to be involved in musical learning and performance, it needs to become a part of the IEP. Once you know that assistive technology would make a difference for students in your class, let the special education teachers know you need the devices. If you aren't sure what types of devices there are and what they do, research what is available virtually or check out a device to try.

One innovative Web-based resource available to music and special educators is the Tub O'Tools. It is a virtual listing of a set of assistive technology devices, equipment, and general software items, contained in a typical storage tub, that meets the needs of a wide range of students with disabilities. (See the following Web site: www.coe.ilstu.edu/seat/tub.htm.) Tub O'Tools does not include specific music hardware or software, but you can see devices that could be used to access both a computer and learning away from the computer such as hardware to mount instruments to wheelchairs.

A more comprehensive Web site may be found at this government sponsored Web site: Abledata (http://www.abledata.com/text2/state_techno logy_assistancejroj.htm). This site includes general information on disabilities, assistive technology information links, location of state Tech Act Projects, equipment resale, and an extensive, searchable database of tens of thousands of assistive technology items and devices. The Illinois Assistive Technology Project is a part of this Tech Act Project list. You can also access it directly at http://www.iltech. org/. Most devices can be taken on loan for four weeks or you can arrange to visit the Project in Springfield to see how the devices work. Contact information is included on the Web site.

Music teachers can arrange a visit to the Illinois Tech Act Project for hands-on opportunities with a range of devices teachers might want to use in their music classes. Short-term borrowing of equipment for trial periods may be available from the Illinois Tech Act Project.

Another helpful site is the RJ Cooper & Associates company, which provides hardware and software for persons with special needs. They have some devices and software that are specific to music, and teachers can download a list of products and software or order a free CD with everything they carry on it (http://www.ricooper.com/). The site is a particular favorite for Macintosh users.

Sometimes seeing how the devices work can help give teachers ideas of different approaches to teaching children with disabilities that do not necessarily require technology. Kolby was successful using the component of Making Music that offered enough visual contrast to see which object to click on. He didn't have to use a computer to see contrast; playing a hand drum with a white head sitting on a black surface would offer the same type of accessibility. Check with the special educator to see if assistive technology is being used in other classes so you can see how it works and how the student uses it. You might be able to borrow the same device for your room, or it might give you an idea for adapting things you already have to help the child participate in music more fully.

One caution in using technology with children with disabilities is to be aware that the child with special needs spends a large portion of the day on a computer. Many children with mild disabilities use a computer to tutor them in weak areas. These children come to know the computer in two ways: the computer means work and usually there is a right way of doing work on the computer, or the computer is a source for playing games. The child with disabilities is painfully aware that he or she is different than other children and most are conscious that they need to figure out a way to get beyond their disabilities to be more like the other kids in school.

When we put them on a computer, they are often so conditioned to focus on finding the right answer that it is difficult for them to use the computer as a means of creating music, an activity that involves divergent ways of thinking. Many children with mild disabilities show signs of learned helplessness. They give up easily or don't even try when they worry that it will be too hard to figure out the right answer. Composing and improvising music might be easier for them when they aren't using a computer. In my experience, using composition software with children with some types of learning disabilities and some types of emotional/behavioral disabilities, I have found that they have a hard time shifting to using the computer in this different way of learning. They didn't show any signs of learned helplessness when they created music on the Soundbeam or the electronic percussion instrument or even working with a small selection of classroom instruments. If you notice students placed on the computer that begin to seem opposed to the task or give up and watch other students working, these are signs of learned helplessness. Students who misbehave when presented with some types of tasks find it much easier to get in trouble and not be allowed to do the activity than to try and fail in front of their peers.

Music teachers are often the busiest people in the school. Our rooms are often physically away from most of the other teachers in the school and we sometimes eat lunch at times when most of the other teachers are having class. This makes it difficult for collaboration between teachers. Collaboration is essential for success for your students with disabilities. You need to find out how to best adapt. Not only is it important to talk to the special educators in the building, but talking with physical education teachers, reading teachers, the school nurse, speech and language specialists, and others, will help you to get a better picture of the child's strengths and weaknesses. When you understand the child better, it will then be easier to advocate for what that child needs in music. All children love music, your charge is to find how to best bring that out in your students.

References

Bryant, B. R., & Seay, P. C. (1998). The Technology-Related Assistance to Individuals with Disabilities Act: Relevance to individuals with learning disabilities and their advocates. *Journal of Learning Disabilities*, 31, 4–15.

Bryant, D. P., & Bryant, B. R. (2003). *Assistive technology for people with disabilities*. Allyn and Bacon: Boston.

Bryant, D. P., Bryant, B. R., & Raskind, M. H. (1998). Using assistive technology to enhance the skills of students with learning disabilities. *Intervention in School and Clinic*, 34, 53–58.

Gregory, D. (2002). Assistive technology for computer-based music instruction. *Journal of Technology in Music Learning*, 1 (2), 15–23.

Individuals with Disabilities Education Act (IDEA), 20 U.S.C. § 1400 et seq. (1997).

Lewis, R.B. (1993). *Special education technology: Classroom applications*. Pacific Grave, CA: Brooks/Cole Publishing Company.

Raskind, M. H., & Higgins, E. L. (1998). Assistive technology for postsecondary students with learning disabilities: An overview. *Journal of Learning Disabilities*, 31, 27–40.

Smith, S. J., & Jones, E. D. (1999). The obligation to provide assistive technology: Enhancing general curriculum access. *Journal of Law and Education*, 28 (2), 247–265.

Technology-Related Assistance for Individuals with Disabilities Act of 1988, 29 U.S.C. § 2201 et. seq. (1988).

This article first appeared in the Spring 2004 issue of the Illinois Music Educator. *Reprinted by permission.*

Inclusion in the Music Classrooms of the Twenty-First Century

Alison Nistad

Before 1975, little legislation existed to protect individuals with disabilities from discrimination in any public setting, be it employment, accessibility, or education. Bernstorf and Welsbacher (1996) report that the Education for All Handicapped Children Act, passed in 1975, stated that,

> To the maximum extent appropriate, handicapped children ... are educated with children who are not handicapped. ... and that special classes, separate schooling, or other removal of handicapped children from the regular school environment occurs only when the nature or severity of the handicap is such that education in regular classes with the use of supplementary aids and services cannot be achieved satisfactorily. (p. 21)

It also declared that the education was to be free and in the "least restrictive environment" (LRE) possible. However, this statement caused a great deal of controversy, as it did not set specific guidelines for the removal of the student from the regular classroom. Another aspect of the act included the creation and implementation of Individualized Educational Programs (IEPs) for each student, and mandated that schooling was to conform to the program set forth in the student's IEP (Damer, 2001).

The next milestone in public policy for the disabled was the passage of the Education of the Handicapped Amendments Act in 1986. The act acknowledged and addressed the need for early intervention programs for children from birth to age two who exhibited developmental delays or conditions that could lead to developmental delays. It also created grants for educational programs for handicapped children from the ages of 3 to 21 (Damer, 2001).

In July of 1990, the Americans with Disabilities Act, a mandate for the "elimination of discrimination against individuals with disabilities" (Damer, 2001, p. 20), was passed. The law became effective in 1992. In October of 1990, additional amendments to the Education of the Handicapped Act of 1975 were passed, widening the range of conditions that would be considered a disability. The act also changed the term "handicapped children" to "children with disabilities" (Damer, 2001, p. 21). It was also declared that IEPs were to contain a statement of transition services that would be used to integrate the student into the outside world after schooling was completed.

The inclusion of the "least restrictive environment" phrase in the 1975 act led to the development of "mainstreaming" students into the normal curriculum. The students would attend regular class for a certain number of hours per day, depending on their tolerance and ability to function in a normal classroom. Oftentimes, to create less disruption for the teacher of academic subjects, students would spend their hours in the regular art, music, or physical education classroom (Warner, 2001).

In the late 1980s, many special educators did not believe that the LRE provision of the act was being followed, and the cost of special education was rising dramatically as better assessment methods were developed and more students were categorized as disabled (Damer, 2001). This led to the Regular Education Initiative, whereby students with disabilities would be integrated into regular classrooms for the entirety of the school day (Damer, 2001). Hence, the term "inclusion" began to be used to refer to the students who were educated in the classroom alongside nondisabled students. These students were provided with support through in-class aides or special pullout sessions, and teachers were able to consult with the special education teacher to discuss specific strategies that would be useful in managing each student.

As Damer (2001) discusses, the U.S. Court of Appeals for the Ninth Circuit heard a case in 1994 and came to the decision that "students are to be placed in regular classroom settings, with the burden of proving that the setting is inappropriate placed on the school system" (p. 22). Inclusion for all students is the goal, but must exist on a continuum with provision for students who cannot be taught effectively in the regular classroom.

One problem that faces the music educator when disabled children are integrated into the classroom is how to create a positive learning environment for both the disabled and nondisabled student. The disabled student must be oriented to classroom rules and procedures in order to function well in the mainstream classroom setting (Zdinksy, 2001). Care must be taken to include the student, even on a limited basis, in all activities the class is completing. It appears that it is often easier to modify the disabled student's participation in a given activity (while still providing a meaningful experience for the student) than it is to modify the entire lesson plan to fit the student.

Partial participation, when the student is only

able to take part in some aspects of the activity, is one common way to include disabled students in the class's activities. "Partial participation must also be meaningful participation that is valued, respected, and performed by peers" (Adamek, 2001, p. 25). Adamek (2001) gives an example of partial participation in her article: a physically disabled student who is unable to participate in a song circle provides a rhythmic accompaniment for the song along with other students. This gives the student an important and necessary role in the group and eliminates the possibility that the student could be humiliated for having a "special" part because he is performing his task with other students.

Musical parts can often be rewritten to meet a disabled student's level of achievement (Adamek, 2001). Rhythms can be simplified, and pitches can be written to fit within the student's range while still maintaining the harmonic integrity of the piece. The student still has an important part to perform, even though it may be simpler than the parts his peers are performing.

It has been shown that educating students in classes that include or are about to include a disabled student is helpful in ensuring they maintain positive attitudes about disabled students (Zdinsky, 2001). A study conducted by Johnson and Darrow (1997) indicated that students who viewed a video containing five instances where a disabled student successfully participated in the regular music classroom had a significantly higher acceptance of disabled students in their classrooms than those who did not view the video.

Music educators must realize that there is support available for them if they have problems or need assistance with integrating the disabled student into their classrooms. Oftentimes, the teacher needs more information as to what strategies are effective in dealing with the student's disability (Humpal and Dimmick, 1995). It is important to stay consistent with rules and procedures that are characteristic of the student's other classes, in order to keep the student in the same frame of mind for music class.

My personal experience this semester with a learning-disabled junior high trombone student, coupled with this research, has taught me that these students have the best intentions but just have difficulty grasping concepts that come easily to other students. This student in particular had been playing for three years, yet did not remember the slide positions for the most basic notes. He often had trouble with finding the exact slide positions. At times, however, he could demonstrate them perfectly one at a time but was unable to link them together for a passage. Praising him for a job well done and then quickly moving on to the next task was an effective technique for working with him, for he was easily distracted and would begin a conversation about an unrelated topic. When he would turn back to the task at hand, it seemed as if all progress made during the lesson had been lost, as he was unfocused and unable to perform the previous exercise accurately.

Inclusion is a topic that has many facets in today's music classroom. Some music educators are resentful and feel that arts classes, as "non-academics," have been used as a dumping ground for disabled students who need to complete a certain number of hours in mainstream classrooms as part of their IEPs. Hopefully, with the resources that are becoming available to today's music educators and the spread of education about disabilities, disabled students will be welcomed into the music classroom by teachers and students alike, for they have many things to share with all who interact with them.

References

Adamek, M. S. (2001). Meeting special needs in music class. *Music Educators Journal*, 87(4), 23–26.

Bernstorf, E. D., & Welsbacher, B. T. (1996). Helping students in the inclusive classroom. *Music Educators Journal*, 82(5), 21–26.

Darner, L. K. (2001). Inclusion and the law. *Music Educators Journal*, 87(4), 19–22.

Humpal, M. E., & Dimmick, J. A. (1995). Special learners in the music classroom. *Music Educators Journal*, 81(5), 21–23.

Johnson, C. M., & Darrow, A. A. (1997). The effect of positive models of inclusion on band students' attitudinal statements regarding the integration of students with disabilities. *Journal of Research in Music Education*, 45(2), 173–184.

Zdinski, S. F. (2001). Instrumental music for special learners. *Music Educators Journal*, 87(4), 27–29, 63.

This article first appeared in the January 2003 issue of New Jersey's Tempo. *Reprinted by permission.*

Inclusion and Lifelong Goals

Peg Ritter

She is 21 now and she calls every Wednesday. If I'm out, she might try again on Thursday or Friday even though she's been told not to call on any other day. Her mother doesn't want her to be a pest! Other adults receive calls from her on those days. Sherrie's elementary years were spent in a segregated elementary school with other students who were educationally mentally handicapped, because she was born with Downs' Syndrome. Mainstreaming brought her to the cluster sites in middle and high school where all her learning was in the special education classroom. She graduated with her age group but knew few of her classmates.

Now she is lonely. True, she works part time in a sheltered workshop and lives with her single mother (who works a couple of jobs) and occasionally gets to church where she collects hugs from a few older people. But her fellow workers seldom call and they never go "mall-shopping" together.

Josie is nearly 22. Increasing back problems now require almost total dependence upon her wheelchair. Yet she takes care of herself quite well in her own small apartment in a building where others who need a bit of watch-care also live. Josie spent elementary years in the same school as Sherrie where she was everyone's friend and her voice brightened our programs. In middle and high school she was mainstreamed along with Sherrie, except she spent more time in regular classrooms, with an IEP demand for an adjusted curriculum in all areas. Her cheerful personality helped develop many friends. At her graduation ceremonies, she rolled triumphantly across the platform to receive her diploma, enjoying the adulation of the crowds.

Today she supplements her SSI income with part-time routine work at a financial institution. She arranges her own transportation, handles her own money, and enjoys many activities with her peers in the limited assistance building where she lives.

About ten years ago, South Dakota mandated that the education of all students with disabilities must be done in their neighborhood schools. Has this been successful? The first of these special learners are now on our streets and in our workplaces, therefore educational researchers are evaluating the results. Because of their concern for academic learning, little attention has been given to music, art, and physical education classes, though these were often the first to be mainstreamed. Still, we can gain from the results of their studies.

First, a few terms, now more clarified:

Mainstreaming. Educating all special learners with their neighborhood peers by selective placement in one or more regular classes.

Inclusion. Defined by each school district in one of these ways:

1. Full-time inclusion of all students with disabilities in the same regular classrooms as they would be if nondisabled, with support services being brought to them there. No necessity to keep up educationally with other students.
2. Full inclusion in regular classes for all, on a part-time basis when needed.
3. Full inclusion for whom it is appropriate. (Some allow special schools.)

Second, troubling difficulties discovered: Researchers indicate that often the inclusion model is chosen to reflect current trends toward total inclusion without regard for the goal of providing "appropriate educational programs for all children." Sadly, some general music teachers say that their classrooms are "full inclusion" even when academic classrooms are not. One teacher reported that eight out of twenty-five students were on IEPs for Learning Disabilities and she only occasionally had assistance! Also, music teachers are seldom involved in placement meetings or have any say as to how many special learners they are to receive.

Third, some successful ideas gleaned from this recent research:

1. Discuss your school's inclusion policy with your administrators.
2. Collaborate closely with special education teachers; request equal time allotment of an educational assistant for your classes. Music is academic, too!
3. If you have an educational assistant, form a CWC (class-within-a-class) so the assistant may adjust what you teach on the level of each special learner.
4. Create sets of easy, quick modification techniques for these learners.
5. A significant number of students on IEPs may give you a right to extra planning time for modifying curriculum. Ask for it ... be bold!
6. Students with emotionally disturbing mental handicaps should not be allowed to disturb other learners. This is a provision of the total plan to "educate *all* learners." You have a right to request removal.
7. Seating arrangements in groups of five with a special learner in each group promotes friendships and assists in learning.

8. A teacher's "up-beat" attitude and excitement about music generates a good learning environment.
9. Share a variety of music for the lifetime enjoyment of your students.
10. Yes, the educational standards *are* important ... for all your students!

Neither Sherrie or Josie were involved in total inclusion. Sherrie's lower mental ability gave little opportunity to be with nondisabled students. Josie's bubbly personality quickly engaged conversation. Yet, the lasting close friendships with nondisabled peers envisioned by inclusion supporters are nonexistent for both girls. Are we setting unrealistic goals? Especially for those with mental deficiencies? Perhaps we are.

Yet, Sherrie feels quite comfortable in her way of life. And Josie? Even with deteriorating health, she enjoys her best friends who are also disabled. Both have many hours of leisure time—most of it spent watching television.

I've never seen lifelong goals for use of leisure time written into an Individualized Education Plan. Maybe they should be!

This article first appeared in the Fall 2000 issue of The South Dakota Musician. *Reprinted by permission.*

Inclusion and the IEP

Peg Ritter

Just as the bell rang, Benny walked solemnly into class and sat in the nearest empty desk. Miss Ann, his educational assistant, whispered that she would return soon. Finding no familiar faces among those glancing his way, he concentrated on the new folder his parents provided just for this class. The room was quiet as the roll was called and he answered with a thick-tongued grin, "That's me, but I'm Benny, not Benjamin!" Every eye was on him and there were smiles and whispers. The teacher looked at him briefly and went on getting acquainted with the other thirty-four names. Benny wondered about all these crowded desks and strange people. Last year, in his special education music class, he would have been warmly welcomed and everyone would have laughed at his witty remarks! Wiggling made his chair squeak ... and everyone looked his way again. So did the teacher, and he knew he should not let a noisy chair bother the class again.

Someone passed him a book. Inside were strange new letters, not like the ABCs he was trying to master. These were circles and sticks with lines going through them. He heard some music but kept paging through his book, looking at the pictures. "Turn to 127," he heard, followed by the rustling of pages by his fellow classmates. What did she say? One-seven? Where are the numbers? On top? No, on the bottom. Here is number one, two, three ... and here is number seven! What a nice picture ... a pretty girl in a swing. Now he heard a song ... something about a chariot coming. What is a chariot? Is it some kind of swing? Some of the kids sang a little. Benny loved to sing. Last year he sang in elementary chorus and he smiled as he thought about it. His special education teachers had helped him learn the songs and told him to sing quietly so others could be heard, too.

The tune bounced along. Soon Benny joined in every time "Good news, chariot's coming" was being sung, except that he usually started too late. Then they all looked at him ... including the teacher. They had told him what her name was, but he couldn't remember. He leaned over to ask the girl next to him, but she just smiled and turned the page in his book to 127. But no one was singing anymore. They were all looking at the chalk-board where the teacher had drawn a bunch of lines with something that held lots of pieces of chalk! Wow! That was a neat trick! Maybe she'd let him try that. He raised his hand to ask, but she was too busy putting sticks and circles all over the lines. She said the students should copy what she wrote, and gave them all some funny paper with the lines too close together for his fat pencil. Everyone began to write, and before he had even written "Benny" on the skinny little lines, the girl across the aisle was finished and had put her pencil down.

He looked at the board. Where should he put the circles? And the sticks? He tried to make some. His circles didn't fit. Where was Miss Ann? What was he supposed to be doing? He looked at the girl across the aisle. "What are we writing?" But she couldn't understand his words. This time he spoke very slowly. "We are writing music," she said. He smiled at her and went on writing circles and sticks all over his paper until the bell rang and Miss Ann came in. "Tomorrow," she said, "I will stay with you and help you." Together they pushed their way down the noisy hall where everyone was trying to beat the three-minute bell to the next class.

Benny thought about his first "regular" seventh grade music class. He liked singing, "Good news, chariot's coming." He liked the nice girl in the row next to him. Someday he hoped he could find the picture of the pretty girl in the swing. Tomorrow he and Miss Ann would write more circles and sticks on the tiny, little lines and call it "music!"

Did Benny have a successful first day in seventh grade music class? If his Individualized Education Plan shows he was placed in the class for (1) social skills, (2) enriched appreciation of music, and (3) new music experiences, this *was* a good day. And there may be few curriculum adaptations needed for future days. However, few IEPs list measurable music education goals, leaving no guidance for adjustment of curriculum, while parents are assuming their child's needs will certainly be met.

Most parents and special education teachers have little awareness of the higher level thinking skills needed to learn music theory. You may find value in preparing a list of activities and academic information needed for your level of music education. Arrange these in order of difficulty from easiest to greatest. At the placement meeting for "Benny," briefly explain each item, suggesting what you see to be necessary for his lifetime of music enjoyment. Together, the choice would be made to require only those academic items deemed beneficial for meeting this goal. Substitute reinforcement skills and enrichment activities while other classmates are doing the more demanding theory. "Benny" will be graded accordingly. This gives you definite guidelines and only that part of the curriculum chosen needs to be adapted.

Before making adaptations, ask for Benny's skill level profile—listing proficiencies in math and reading, and for behavior and social skills. See if there are general IEP goals that could be monitored by the educational assistant provided to help Benny.

A few standard supplementary aids can be used for most inclusion students in the regular music class.

1) Provide a pocket-type folder containing these items (securely fastened to the inside cover when possible):
   a) a simple notation chart of notes, rests, their names, and time value in 4/4 time
   b) a line/space cue card
   c) a picture syllable chart of hand signs
   d) a list of terms using simple definitions/pictures
2) Always write page numbers in a certain place so the student knows where to look for it.
3) Most-used songs can be copied, enlarged, highlighted. Songs may be taped and sent home to be learned.
4) Provide larger-lined staff paper for those who have writing difficulties.
5) Tests: Reduce number of questions; rewrite in easier words; be sure printing is clear and plain; allow student pretest study and extra time to take the test; have the assistant give test orally or on tape.

The South Dakota Department of Special Education indicates that "to the maximum extent appropriate ... the regular classroom in the school the student would attend if not disabled is the *first* placement option considered before a more restrictive placement is considered, ... with supplementary aids and services provided." Only "if the student's IEP cannot be implemented in this environment may another placement be considered." This is not a change in the Individuals with Disabilities Education Act, but a more exact interpretation of it.

So ... move over, Benny! You may soon be joined by others from your special education classroom ... and you can enjoy seventh grade music education together!

This article first appeared in the Spring 1995 issue of The South Dakota Musician. *Reprinted by permission.*

Reaching All Students

Peg Ritter

"Oh, yes, I remember him well!" Ms. Merri Musik joined her fellow staff members in the faculty lounge. "It was my first year of teaching music and I was nearly overwhelmed by the variety of age groups and sheer numbers of students streaming in and out of my room! He was the only one to stop by my desk and talk to me. I still remember his shy words: 'Hi, I'm Lon. I liked your music class today!' and he was out the door. That brightened my whole day!"

The teachers were discussing Lon's recent visit to the school to "touch base" with his former teachers whom he regarded as his "best friends."

The art teacher chimed in, "I remember him as a quiet boy who always chose the back row but never caused any trouble."

"He never excelled in any sport," added the gym teacher. "But he filled his spot the best he could."

"Schoolwork was always a struggle for him, and he said no one at home could help him," remarked the language arts teacher. "But I had an overload of students that year. There just wasn't time to help him very much!"

Merri agreed, "He enjoyed listening to music and singing, but the music theory was a constant confusion for him. Sadly, I hadn't yet learned the skills for adjusting music curriculum that I use now."

"Lon told me today that he's about to graduate," the shop teacher said as he reached for another bagel.

"Oh, but he should have graduated more than a year ago," this from the school secretary. "He dropped out a couple of times, then kept asking to try again. It's so important to him to get that diploma. I hope he makes it this time! I'm really concerned about him!"

Then another teacher stood to get their attention. "I've got an idea! Let's be his tutors this spring. He could stop in here after his classes are over and if we all share a bit of time, we might be able to ..."

Just then the principal entered, filled his cup with fresh coffee and smiled. "I always knew you were the best teachers ever! I heard your great idea, and I'll help, too. And to assist you in your endeavor, I've just contacted one of those educational research groups to teach our in-service sessions. This group targets those ranking in the lower half of the academic achievement curve. They begin with the premise that most of our students will never get into that top percentage of our class which usually gets all the acclaim."

At the first session, Ms. Musik and her colleagues were amazed by a few statistics:

- In the last 30–40 years more scientific information has been learned than in the previous 5000 years.
- Scientific information now doubles every 4–5 years.
- General information doubles every 5–7 years.
- Today's technology will be outdated in about 5 years (From *US News and World Report*, 12/99).

The teachers were told that much of the information they were taught during their public school years is already outdated. Today's students must not only absorb the basics their teachers learned, but add the daily increase of today's knowledge. For the struggling learner, this appears formidable! The research presenters added that teachers tend to favor brighter students. Then came the clincher: the big push for academic excellence with its resultant publication of test scores and their corresponding rating of schools places tremendous pressure on teachers! And often it's "low-scoring students" who are blamed. This tends to create negative attitudes toward that large percentage of students who may never excel in anything.

Then DOs and DON'Ts began to fly into the teachers' notebooks:

DO see that the lower 25 percent your class is as important as upper 25 percent.

DON'T list test grades on the board from highest to lowest. Always being on the bottom is tough!

DO emphasize that their own degree of improvement is more important than being on top!

Let them know you empathize with their struggle.

DON'T discourage students with harsh, sarcastic language and disapproving nonverbals.

Catch them behaving appropriately and acknowledge what they do *right*!

DO find ways to assist them, and help them feel included and valued. Send notes of recognition and publicize their successes.

DO greet students daily with a feeling of your confidence in what they *can* do.

DO discover when these students may need more help then you can give them and assist them through the process—go with them if necessary. At least 5 percent of today's students are plagued with Attention Deficit Hyperactivity Disorder (ADHD).

DO keep in mind that anxiety disorders are the most frequent health problems for 9–17 year-olds. Twenty percent of these children have mental health and learning disorders that can be diagnosed and treated. Depression treatment in children has an 80 percent success rate. Yet, remember this—suicide is the third leading cause of death in 15–25-year-olds and the fourth leading cause among 10–14-year-olds.

DO consistently discover new methodology for reaching all students—particularly this lower half.

DO insist that students take the initiative to learn—with the promise of your help: a winning team!

DO your best as a teacher; if you can't reach them all today, do the best you can! Your struggling students need to know you really care! You may be the only one who does!

Summer had come and at the end of the last day Ms. Merri spotted a note on the teacher's bulletin board: "Dear Teachers, Thank you for being my friends. I decided to try once more and if I didn't make it this time, life wouldn't hold anything good for me anymore. But you kept calling me, sending me notes to make me feel good, and helping me with the tough lessons. Just wanted you to know that *this time I made it!* I got my *diploma* last night. Your very thankful friend, Lon."

This article first appeared in the Spring 2001 issue of The South Dakota Musician. *Reprinted by permission.*

Eight Classroom Strategies for Working with ADD/ADHD Children: A Guide for Teachers and Parents

Harry R. Robe

Introduction

Much information about hyperactivity has been gained in the past few years. It is now understood that this is a problem caused by brain differences in about 10 percent of the children currently attending school and not a problem caused by poor parenting skills or child abuse. The ratio of boys to girls who are diagnosed as ADHD or ADD, is about four to one, although the higher incidence of diagnosed ADHD in boys is probably due to the more aggressive nature of boys. Actually, the number of girls with ADHD is probably about the same as boys; the condition is just expressed differently, and girls are not diagnosed as often.

In recent years, there has been an increase in the incidence of diagnosed ADHD as well as an increase in the diagnosis of other disorders, such as OCD (Oppositional Child Disorder) learning disabilities, and emotional problems among children such as childhood depression.

One of the more controversial aspects of the diagnosis and treatment of ADHD has been the rapid increase in the prescription of Ritalin and other stimulant medications. At the present, there are at least 25 prescription medications which have been found to be of some help with ADHD children. Although different medications, in different dosage levels and administration patterns, have been found to be effective in aiding children with problems of distractibility, attention, impulsivity, and hyperactivity, no medication has been found which treats the learning problems children have at school which often accompany or are caused by ADD or ADHD.

This article has been developed as an educational treatment after the diagnosis and medication treatment for ADHD. Many of these suggestions help with behavior control in the classroom, but are also techniques for enhancing a child's learning potential in the classroom. In fact, most children diagnosed as borderline to mild ADHD or moderate ADHD can be effectively treated without medication by using the suggestions in this article. Those children with severe ADHD almost always need medication as well as the suggestions offered here.

I. Managing the ADHD Child at School

School, with its demands for order, neatness, task completion, quiet, and discipline is often the place where the ADHD child has the greatest difficulties. The unpredictable, disruptive, aggressive, and erratic classroom performance of the ADHD child makes teaching difficult. The symptoms of the ADHD child as seen in school are:

1. Does not stay in his/her seat; wiggles and moves about.
2. Talkative, speaks out of turn, talks while working.
3. Does not pay attention to directions.
4. Will not complete his/her work.
5. Messy, loses work, misplaces pencils, paper, books, etc.
6. Overly aggressive, hits, pushes, will not stay in line.
7. Creates problems in the gym, library, on the playground, on the bus, in restrooms, in hall ways, and when supervised by a substitute teacher.
8. Moody, "in his/her own world," frequently off task, lies, copies from others, takes things from others.

Any one child may or may not exhibit these behaviors, and the severity of the problems will vary greatly from child to child, and for the same child from day to day. Often, school seems to be the only place where the child's problems are recognized and it is implied that the teacher is the problem, not the child.

The ADHD child is described most frequently as being "immature' because of his/her nonconforming and problematic behaviors. He/she is often seen as a bright and capable child who "can do the work but won't!" Neither of these amateur diagnoses is accurate or helpful. The diagnosis of "immaturity" only leads to delay of treatment, as it implies that all the child needs to do is to "grow up," and either placing the child in a slow track or retaining the child is all that needs to be done for the problem to go away. Seeing the child as "willful or disobedient" leads to excessive use of punishment and loss of self-esteem for the child. Working with these children is very frustrating for teachers as the usual strategies don't seem to help, and teachers often feel that they get little or no support from others.

Because of the complex political, economic, and social structure of the school systems, the bureaucracy, teachers also feel that they get little support from within the schools. ADHD has not been recognized as a "special education category," and teachers cannot get the help they need from the specialists within the schools. In order to avoid possible liability for treatment costs, most schools declare that ADHD is a medical, not an educational problem, and have no provisions for help for teachers. It is only when an ADHD child is given a secondary diagnosis of mental retardation, behavior disorder (emotional disturbance), or learning disability that help is made available from special classes and special education teachers. Retaining a child in grade is often the only solution which seems to be available, and when that is done, it does not help in most instances. Actually, retention often makes matters worse, as then the child is older, larger, stronger, and is angry in response to a loss of self-esteem. Retention is often vigorously opposed by parents as the child's problem is that he/she does not do the work, not that the child has not learned the material. In supervising homework, parents are aware that the real problem is production, not learning.

II. Developing Some Management/ Teaching Strategies for Working with the ADHD Child in the Classroom

It takes a coordinated effort which involves not only the teacher and child, but school support personnel, parents, and professionals to develop successful strategies for working with ADHD children. For teachers, the key to success is building good working relationships with the child and the child's parents. If things have gotten off to a bad start, it is often necessary for teachers to be the leaders in rebuilding relationships which have gone bad. It is often necessary to remind oneself that the child is not the problem, the child has a problem. Be calm and patient and do not expect the problem to go away or be cured by any one simple thing you can do. There is no cure for ADHD, only strategies which can make the child's life more meaningful and successful.

Begin by making an inventory of the child's assets and liabilities, strengths and weaknesses. Talk with the child's parents and with the child to cooperatively decide what a child can and cannot do. If there are missing data, seek help from school personnel, or ask the parents to do so with out-of-school professionals.

Divide the responsibilities for collecting data and observations among the child's significant adults. Develop a timeline for action and set a time for a planning session. Plan for periodic follow-up sessions. Before making final decisions, cooperatively gather information which will answer the following questions:

1. What are the similarities and differences in the child's behavior patterns in school and out of school?
2. Does the child qualify for a diagnosis of ADD or ADHD?
3. Does the child have other developmental or behavioral problems which are causes of the child's problems, or make the child's ADD or ADHD more difficult to manage?
4. What treatments or strategies have been tried at school or at home? Has medication been considered or tried? If so, what were the observed effects? What is the present homework supervision and general strategy for schoolwork support which is being used at home?
5. Are there identifiable patterns of behavior, such as afternoons better or worse than mornings, Mondays better than Fridays, days before or after vacations or holidays different from routine days, etc.?
6. Who are the people who are involved with this child's case, parents, relatives, tutors, psychologists, social workers, pediatricians, counselors, and special teachers, and what part or role does each play?

Once the data have been collected and more is known about this child's particular patterns of strengths, weaknesses and behaviors, tentative decisions can be made concerning classroom arrangements, instructional guidance, and follow-up activities. Keep in mind that there is no simple set of changes which will cure the problem. A good rule of thumb is that a perfect program will work for about two weeks at a time, and then adjustments will have to be made.

III. The Child in the Classroom

1. The two best alternatives for seating the child in the classroom are to (a) seat the child in the middle of the last row in the classroom, or (b) seat the child near the teacher's desk. With the majority of ADHD children, the seat in the back of the classroom is the best, as there the child is not "stimulus deprived" and does not have to turn around or be concerned with sounds and actions which cannot be seen. Also, the child will always be in the teacher's line of sight as she moves about the classroom, and visual contact can be maintained with the child. For a few "over-stimulated" children, the seat next to the teacher's desk works best. When a trial decision on seating is made, plan to test the arrangement for at least two weeks before trying something else. Give the child time to adapt to his/her place, and avoid changes as much as possible.
2. Do not place the child in the line of traffic or near distracting stimuli such as doors, windows, air conditioners, or near the hallway door.
3. It is sometimes useful to have a "quiet work place" in a low traffic, low noise part of the room which is available for all children, including the ADHD child. It is sometimes useful to have padded ear phones and a source of taped, nonstimulating, quiet background music so the child who is in the "quiet place" can screen out distracting sounds while working. Some visual screening is also sometimes useful, but be careful with too much screening for the ADHD child as he/she becomes more agitated when deprived of auditory or visual stimuli.
4. Avoid abrupt transitions as ADHD children often do not handle transitions well. "Program" the child when change is coming up. Quietly go over the requirements of the next activity, such as what is going to happen in the gym or in the lunchroom, and review the general requirements of the next activity. "Program" the child in a quiet, private, supportive way. Take a moment to talk with the child, often touching his/her shoulder and semi-whispering the "program" for the next activity. Avoid open classroom scolding or reprimanding of the ADHD child. The child's principal teacher should take time to plan with the other teachers who work with the child. Do not require the child to make adaptations as he/she goes from one setting to another or from one teacher to another. Personality transitions are as difficult as activity transitions.
5. Sometimes ADHD children need a safety valve, a way of getting away from pressures when the pressures get too great. When the teacher or child becomes aware that pressure is building up, arrangements can be made for a place of retreat or sanctuary for a child. A table in the corner of the library, a work space in the counselor's office, a place in the school office area, or sometimes even an arrangement with the teacher next door for the child to slip quietly into another classroom to work. A quiet, visual signal system can be worked out between teacher and child when the safety valve is needed.

IV. Giving Instructions and Making Assignments

1. Help the child become an "active listener" when assignments are being given. Develop a "talking" and "listening" silent, visual signal which can pass back and forth between teacher and ADHD child. A teacher placing his/her finger on a cheek, answered by the child placing his/ her finger on a cheek before starting verbal instructions signals a talking-listening episode. Use the same set of signals to end the episode. Most ADHD children maintain very poor eye contact, and as long as they know when an episode starts and ends, constant, forced eye contact may be a distraction instead of an aid.
2. Occasionally have the ADHD child "pass on" the instructions to another child by going over to another child and whispering the instructions to that child when signaled to do so by the teacher. This serves two important purposes. First, it allows the child to vocally restate the instructions before starting, thereby clarifying the instructions, and secondly, the child will be an active listener instead of a passive listener; and even though not always getting to pass on the instructions, will learn to listen as if he/she is to vocalize the instructions. A variation of this procedure is to occasionally have the ADHD child paraphrase the instructions orally to the class when signaled to do so. This should

not be something which is done only by the ADHD child, but other children should also be asked to do this, especially children who present a good model for the ADHD child.

3. Another active listening device is to provide the child with some 3 x 5 cards, and when instructions have been given, have the child write down the main ideas on the card and quietly place the card on the teacher's desk. When the child has completed the assignment, he/she can quietly pick up the card and initial or project a grade for the work on the card and place it back on the teacher's desk. This procedure establishes a clear start and stop time for assignments. Avoid having the child put start and stop times on the card as this encourages impulsivity, one of the child's major problems.
4. As a part of the positive relationship building with the child, help the ADHD child feel comfortable when seeking help with instructions or assignments. Most ADHD children when they don't understand what to do, rather than ask for help, impulsively quit and start doing something else such as playing with pencils or toys or talking. They often ask "global" questions like, "What is it I'm supposed to do?" which are irritants to the teacher and draw short replies. Teach them to ask specific questions about those things which they don't understand, sometimes cueing them with possible questions until they learn how to ask their questions.
5. Make instructions clear and concise. Be consistent with the way instructions are given. Restate and simplify complex instructions (multistep instructions), and whenever possible, avoid multiple commands.
6. Give out only one task at a time. Multiple pages and multiple instructions overwhelm the ADHD child, and they "turn off" and impulsively do something else or rush through without taking time to be careful and correct.
7. Give the child some form of immediate feedback upon completion of an assignment. A "qualify" or "appearance" grade is easy and quick to give and does not require reading or checking the paper at the time it is turned in. One simple system is to have three kinds of colored paper tickets in order on the teacher's desk. One color could mean "very good," another "good," and the third, "not so good." As the papers are turned in, the teacher could quietly say, "red,"etc., and the child would pick out the ticket and place it in a collection at his/ her desk for later cumulated rewards or praise.
8. An often useful technique is to teach the ADHD child to use a highlighter pen to mark operative phrases in instructions or critical words when listening to instructions or surveying work pages before starting to work. When an impulsive child has a pencil in his/her hand, he/she often just begins without reading instructions or noting details. Using the highlighter delays this impulsive start and reduces errors.

V. When the Student Is Performing Assignments

1. Monitor the child's work frequently. ADHD children have a short attention span and impulsively quit working or become careless if they are on their own too long at a time. There are several easy, nonintrusive ways to work with the child while the child is working on assignments. One is to show the child how to divide the long assignment into "chunks," approximately fourths, and exchange silent visual signals as each chunk is complete. ("Give me our signal when you have finished each chunk, and you know you have done it right.") Another way is have the child identify on his/her paper the hardest problem or task on the page before starting work. Then have the child work that problem and show it to the teacher, occasionally explaining how he/she knows it is correct, before completing the assignment.
2. Be sure that assignments are learning exercises and are testing skills and knowledge rather than attention span. A few examples with some form of immediate feedback are much more valuable as learning episodes than longer assignments with no or delayed feedback for success. Select, or help the child to select, the critical parts of an assignment and have those parts worked first, thus ensuring that the critical parts are completed with the more repetitive "practice" being the part which is undone or neglected if any part is neglected.
3. Have the ADHD child turn in each assignment as it is completed, receive immediate feedback in some form, and then go on to additional work. Be sure the child knows what to do next, and encourage clarification as needed.
4. Teach the child how to keep records of assignments as made and completed. Include in the assignment records the child's estimate of his/ her grade on the assignment at the time it is completed, and the actual grade when the paper is returned with the teacher's grade and comments. A daily card taped to the child's desk is

probably more adaptive than a notebook chart (which the ADHD child will probably lose). A form card for the children's use can easily be duplicated and made available for each day. Each child can hang the cards on the board at the end of each day. If the child has incomplete assignments, the card can be taken home along with the books or materials needed and returned with the work the next day. A bright red tag can be hung on the board chart to remind the child if the card is returned the next day. At the end of the week, the teacher has an accounting of the quality and completeness of the card records and some form of praise or reward given for good records, a form for positive discipline, not just assertive discipline.

5. Remember that ADHD children have very poor frustration tolerance and become easily frustrated and agitated, going off task easily. Stress, pressure, and fatigue can break down a child's self-control and lead to problem behavior. Break up desk work sessions with some kind of opportunity for activity. With the more severe level ADHD child, having the chance to go outside and run around the playground once or a similar activity before starting the next desk work session is often helpful.
6. Be flexible with time demands. Give extra time for certain tasks. Because they have difficulty in focusing their attention, ADHD children often work inefficiently and more slowly than other children. Try not to penalize the extra time which is needed. Be very careful with timed demands, as ADHD children over-respond and have more difficulty with focus and attention when they are concerned with the clock. If a task is to be timed, give the child a "half-way" signal, so he/she has the opportunity to adjust the pace and have some knowledge of the rate of time passage, rather than timing from just the start time to stop time.

VI. Recommendations for Supervision and Discipline

1. When there is a rule infraction or disturbance, remain calm. State the infraction and don't argue or debate with the child. Avoid the "Why" question and ask instead, "What did you do?" Ask the child to be descriptive, not evaluative. Be patient, don't force or demand responses or apologies on the spot. Say, "I know this is hard to describe, go back to work and in a little while we'll talk about it." Allow some time for the stress of the moment to dissipate before trying to arrive at corrective action or administering discipline.
2. Have clear, rational, cooperatively agreed upon rules and consequences for misbehavior. Administer consequences which fit the crime, without harshness, hostility, ridicule, or criticism.
3. Be consistent in the identification of misbehavior and administration of consequences. Just because the ADHD is often the "squeaky wheel," don't always assume that talking or noises have come from that child. Avoid overuse of the child's name. ADHD children often hear their name called so often that they become desensitized in hearing their name and impulsively go on with their activities. Learn to use hand signals to communicate with the ADHD child.
4. Avoid openly and publicly reminding students on medication to "take your medicine" or asking, "Did you take your medicine today?" especially when there has been an incident of misbehavior or a rule infraction. Do not make medication any more of an issue with the ADHD child than with any other child with a medical or neurological problem, like seizures, asthma, or diabetes. Respect the child's privacy, especially in the eyes of his/her peers.
5. Don't use spanking or other means of administering physical pain as "discipline" methods with the ADHD child. Divert the child, plan with the child, use the child's safety valve as a time-out to reduce stress and tension before trying to talk with the child or reason with the child.
6. Be extremely careful that the child is not stigmatized, categorized, or that others prejudge or are prejudiced toward the child. Let the child start out with a "clean slate" when entering into new situations or moving on to new teachers. Avoid the use of labels or "diagnoses" when talking to others about the child.

VII. Providing Encouragement and Positive Guidance

1. Make sure the child is praised, noticed, helped, and rewarded more than he/she is punished, in order to build positive self-esteem.
2. Find ways of noticing and providing positive feedback for good behavior and effort.
3. Teach the child to reward himself/herself. Model and encourage positive self-talk, such as "You must be very proud of yourself, the way you stayed in your seat today. Being able to finish that whole paper must make you feel very good. Remembering to bring in your homework today must make you feel great!" Minimize

statements which imply that the child is working to make others feel good and be proud, emphasize that the child does the right thing because it makes him/her feel good. "You must be impressed with the way you handled that" is much more positive than, "I'm impressed, etc."

4. If you are aware that some intended reward is not working (does not reinforce), change rewards. Be a good observer and creatively discover what works and does not work. Sharing observations with parents and others who work with the child is helpful.
5. Be genuine and honest. ADHD children are very perceptive of feelings and recognize when someone is faking it with them.

VIII. Other Recommendations Which May Be Useful

1. Additional educational, psychological, and neurological evaluation is sometimes useful in finding more about learning style, patterns of cognitive ability and ruling out the possibility of learning disabilities and neurological problems.
2. Private, one-on-one instruction is often helpful, as ADHD children frequently work very well in the more focused and verbal one-on-one situation.
3. Teacher personalities and styles make a big difference. Generally, the verbal, creative, supportive teacher is better than the more task oriented, "disciplinarian" teacher. Sometimes it is useful to think carefully about which classes or with which teachers the child might work better.
4. Some kind of social skills training and study skills or organizational skills training is helpful. A more formal kind of therapy called "cognitive behavior modification" has been shown to be effective with many ADHD children. Professional therapists who have training in cognitive behavior modification should be identified as resources.
5. Many ADHD children like gimmicks and gadgets; computers and using a word processor are often good ways of getting school work done. Word processors are very useful with the child who has problems with handwriting and visual-motor development.
6. ADHD children often do poorly in highly competitive team sports. Individualized activities that are mildly competitive or self-competitive, such as bowling, tennis, walking, track, biking, or karate drain off excess energy and are good esteem builders. Also, individual activities involve more flexible scheduling and allow for more individualization and less conformity.
7. Introducing the child to social activities, such as scouting, church groups, Big Brothers/Sisters programs, and other child or youth organizations helps with the development of social skills.
8. The ADHD child should be allowed freedom to try different age groups and play groups, finding where they fit in. Many ADHD children play better with younger children and have more in common with younger children. The child can still develop valuable social skills from interactions with younger children, where he/she can play on their level.
9. A discipline strategy known as "response cost" which involves a process of "earning" or "losing" rewards in a visible, continuous way is often useful. Promises of long-term or large rewards just don't work. Impulsive children work in the immediate, and although they may seem to enjoy the idea of the "big reward" for long-term changes or improvements, the enthusiasm soon wears off. Daily, or sometimes hour-to-hour, or moment-to-moment concrete tokens or objects are usually most effective.

Suggested Readings and References

Barkley, Russell; *Attention Deficit Hyperactivity Disorder*, New York: Guildford Press 1990 (somewhat technical, but the best!).

Barkley, Russell; *Defiant Children: A Clinician's Manual for Parent Training* New York: Guildford Press 1989.

Garber, et al.; *Your Child is Hyperactive. Inattentive. Impulsive, Distractable* ..., New York: Villard Books 1990 (simplified guide for parent).

Sunday Gazette Mail, "Inaccuracies about Ritalin," John Wender, MD, January 10, 1988, Charleston, West Virginia.

CHADD: Children With Attention Deficit Disorders, 1859 N. Pine Island Road, Suite 185, Plantation, FL 33322; (305) 792-8100 or 384-6869. (A parent-professional support and information group with many resources for teachers and parents.)

Attention Deficit Disorders: A Guide for Teachers an informative pamphlet prepared by the Education Committee of CHADD Nov. 1988.

This article first appeared in the October 1996 issue of Kentucky's Bluegrass Music News. *Reprinted by permission.*

Reaching Students with Special Needs

Michael Ross

In this new millennium, a primary challenge will be the ability to successfully teach all of our students. To some teachers, this challenge seems insurmountable. But we often relish the task of preparing enriched activities for our most gifted students. It only seems a challenge to work with those at a different end of the spectrum. I feel strongly that we must meet this challenge head on; it is our moral imperative to teach, respect, and cherish every student that enters our classroom(s).

A colleague recently shared a story concerning a year that she taught a special ed pull-out music class. The classroom teacher in whose room she was teaching would have nothing to do with "those" kids. She would walk in after class, holding her nose (while the students were still in the room), and open the windows. It is this type of story shared by my colleague that reminds me of our moral imperative to care about all of our students. And even though working with some students sometimes seems a special challenge, so be it: we have successes and failures with all of our students. Here are a few of my successes and failures—perhaps you will recognize your own experiences in these stories, or perhaps they will be new to you.

Sam

Sam, who is blind, came to me as a very shy freshman to audition for the vocal jazz class. He sang very softly (and accurately) with a tape. He was the first student I had taught who had a visual impairment, and I was excited and nervous about this new teaching challenge. Sam, who also has a mild cognitive disability, did not read braille well, so I made him tapes of the songs we were learning. I quickly saw him grow from a shy freshman to one of the most popular students in choir. Today, Sam still sings in the vocal jazz ensemble but also is a member of our auditioned concert choir. In that ensemble, he works with a student partner who helps him learn the music and get around the choir room. I feel strongly that Sam's experience in choir was a successful one, and I have learned much from working with him.

John

John was a student with a cognitive disability who sang in my vocal jazz ensemble. He started the semester "slowly," often seeming tired and uninterested during class. (Although he was usually happy to share his enthusiasm for the Green Bay Packers.) Throughout the semester, I saw John's passiveness turn to active interest. He learned all of the songs with the ensemble and sang with us at the concert. Did he know all of the words or even the melodies? No. But the look of sheer bliss on his face was enough for me to know this experience had been successful.

Lorraine

My experiences with differently-abled students have not always been as successful as those noted above. Sometimes, a lack of communication or goals left unclear hinder the situation. Currently I have a student, Lorraine, who has autism. She comes to class daily with a special education assistant (SEA). Lorraine is sometimes violent with her SEA, hitting her on the arm when confronted with a new situation or when frustrated with what is going on in class. Her interest in music is clear; she often sings with great enthusiasm (and skill). But I feel that her time during class is not entirely successful. I often interact with her indirectly during class, relying instead on the SEA present. I rarely communicate with her case manager or her parents.

David

I have another student in my choral program, David, who also has autism. I did not know this until he told me in passing six weeks into the semester! On the surface, that would seem remarkable; he is able to be fully included in all class activities. But he often talks out of turn, has awkward social skills, and asks questions many times. I grew frustrated with his behavior, as did most of the students in the class. It was David's revelation that helped to remind me of my responsibility to work with all of my students. Since then, I have slowly attempted to change my interactions with him. Unfortunately, I still revert to old habits easily and am often too impatient with David.

Although I am not always successful in teaching students with special needs, I still cherish the experiences I have had (and will continue to have) with them. Frankly, my experiences with students with special needs reflect my experiences with all of my students; sometimes I teach well, and other times I teach poorly. Either way, I try to work hard teaching all of my students. This is our challenge in the new millennium.

This article originally appeared in the February 2001 issue of the Wisconsin School Musician. *Reprinted by permission.*

Justin's Story

William Santoro, MD

I always had something against home movies where parents put their children on display. You would hear the parent behind the camera telling the child, "Honey do your trick for the camera." One of my hobbies is photography. I took a lot of still photos until I became a parent, then I added videotaping to my hobby. I made a promise to myself and to the world; I would not direct the film, I would simply be an observer, and record it. I never thought how important this little promise would become.

Justin, our first child, was a beautiful baby. I have the proof in pictures and video for anyone to see. I also have videotaped evidence that he was perfectly normal in every way. The subject of whether, and when, our son was diagnosed with autism remains debatable. Jill and I noticed that there was something different about Justin when he was just 18 months old. His language did not seem to be progressing as we expected. At that time, professionals would not make a diagnosis of autism until the age of three. We also had a healthy dose of denial to help hide our concern.

Our pediatrician recommended several specialists. One of them told us *we* were the problem; others told us there was *no* problem at all. Justin scored very low on the IQ test—so low, in fact, that we had to question the results. We were informed that Justin was given a verbal IQ test because he was too young to read. My wife and I pointed out to the therapist that she had just administered a verbal IQ test to a child whose problem is language. Jill and I made another promise; in order to test or treat *our* child, a therapist had to have a child of his or her own.

It took my profession 18 months to give us even a clue as to what we were dealing with. Then came the well-meaning relatives who claimed they knew something was different about Justin from the day he was born. They told us he didn't look at them or interact with them, even as an infant. My 12 hours of unedited, undirected, and unrehearsed videotapes showed that Justin was indistinguishable from any other child until he was 18 months old.

What Jill and I needed at that time in our lives was support, understanding, and unconditional love for our child. What we often got were statements about how everyone else knew what the problem was before we did. One of the best pieces of advice we received came from an occupational therapist turned psychologist who told us we could be depressed over lost dreams, or we could celebrate the beautiful and unique child we had.

Our first introduction to therapy was "play therapy." Play therapy seemed to us to be exactly what we did with Justin, as parents, in our everyday lives. We were also sent to the Easter Seal Society and introduced to occupational therapy. The therapist combined these two modalities beautifully. Shortly afterwards, music therapy was recommended.

Justin did well with occupational and play therapy. Jill and I also felt that Justin needed what we called "social therapy." He liked to be around people and tried to make friends, but could not understand how to go about it. Justin had a videotape about a boy who was the new child on the block. The video showed how this boy made friends with other children. Justin watched it repeatedly, almost as if it were a training tape. He especially enjoyed the recorded music.

Justin received his first formal music therapy through the Easter Seal Society. I am not going to describe what the therapist did in music therapy. That would be like a fan describing what a basketball player does on a basketball court. What I *will* concentrate on is what music therapy did for Justin, and for us.

Music therapy started with the piano and keyboard. Our first music therapist left the Easter Seals Society for private practice. When the Easter Seals Society did not replace her, we took Justin to her studio for private music therapy. It was here that she noticed his fascination with the violin. For a short time, she used the violin as a reward. It quickly became apparent that the violin worked better than the keyboard as the main instrument for Justin's therapy. Music therapy gave Justin a new sensation on which to concentrate. I also believe the violin, in particular, gave him a vibratory sensation that he found enjoyable. Music therapy evolved into music lessons and today, Justin continues playing the violin in high school. He plays a lot by ear and has an uncanny ability to play what his instructor plays as it is played for the first time. Justin did so well with the violin that it was appropriate for him to have his own. We are fortunate to live in the same town as a world-renowned violin maker. Mr. Fegley would not sell anyone a violin without interviewing the customer first. Jill arranged a one-hour meeting with him to talk to Justin. Jim Fegley was also one of the most accepting people Jill had ever met. At that meeting Mr. Fegley brought out many violins for Justin to try. He was allowed to play each one and to get a feel for the violins. Mr. Fegley questioned him about the feel and the sound. Justin kept coming back to one violin in particular. Jill agreed to buy the violin Justin chose, and asked Mr. Fegley if Justin had made a good choice. Mr. Fegley told her that, of the five final violins Justin narrowed his choice to, two of them, including the one he finally chose, were made by him. Mr. Fegley said it with such obvious pride. Jill said he seemed honored to have Justin playing one of his handcrafted violins.

We do not know where Justin gets his musical ability, certainly not from me. He has perfect pitch and likes his violin perfectly tuned. This presents a problem because neither Jill nor I can tune the violin to his satisfaction. Once, Jill took the violin to a music store and asked a staff member to tune it. The store was crowded and the young worker seemed uninterested in helping Justin. Justin was being Justin and making some strange noise while moving his arms in such a way as to bring the attention of several customers. Jill ignored the stares (we have simply gotten used to them). Again, Jill asked the "expert" to tune the violin. The person at the counter played the violin and told her it was practically in perfect tune. Jill said, "I know it is almost perfectly tuned, *now* make it perfect." Obviously disgusted, he tuned it and handed it back to Jill. The last thing Jill was going to do was drive home and find that it was not tuned properly; so she handed the violin to Justin and asked him to check it. Justin put the violin under his chin and rapidly fired off a classical piece. When he was finished, Jill asked him if the instrument had been properly tuned. Justin said it was and, as they turned to leave, Jill realized there was not a sound in the store. Justin's impromptu performance had mesmerized everyone. It is what Jill calls an "E.F. Hutton moment."

Sometimes, music therapy drifts into other types of therapy. In speech therapy one day, the teacher was having a little trouble keeping Justin interested in a discussion of the four seasons. The lesson began with a simple question, "Justin, what are the four seasons?" Justin ignored him. The therapist asked several more times, "Justin, can you tell me what are the four seasons?" Still, Justin ignored him. Finally, the frustrated therapist intoned, "Justin, you are not leaving here until you answer me. Now, what are the four seasons?" With an impish grin, Justin quietly answered, "They're concertos by Vivaldi."

Until he turned 10, Jill shouldered the burden of managing Justin's therapies alone. I justified this by saying I was busy building a medical practice. Sometimes I wonder if, subconsciously, I avoided helping because the emotional strain was, at times, overwhelming. Like a child wanting to learn to swim but afraid to jump into the water, I wanted to help. The first time I considered voice lessons was when Justin, at a young age, sang "Happy Birthday." He would sing loudly and cover his ears because he did not like hearing others singing out of tune. I told Jill I wanted Justin to take voice lessons. She told me if it was going to happen, it would be up to me. When Justin was a little older, I jumped into the water, and took him to his first voice lesson. It was a disaster but, in the end, we *both* got our feet wet.

Justin has a very dry sense of humor. He also quickly learns what pushes a person's buttons. He *loves* to imitate people. Justin's first voice tutor had a slight British accent that he naturally picked up on. This teacher was very rigid in her lessons. She wanted Justin to listen to her sing first, and then repeat when she commanded. Justin would sing with her immediately.

He could sing, in tune and in her accent, a song he was hearing *her* sing for the first time. She never believed this and kept saying he must have heard the song before. Justin was devastated when, after a few months of lessons, the teacher told me (in Justin's presence) that he should pick another hobby. The teacher felt Justin would *never* be able to sing well. She never understood that we were not looking for our son to be a professional. She never understood that this was a child who spoke very few words due to a language problem. She never understood that this was my *child*, with whom I would do *anything* to hold a conversation. For Justin, singing was the closest thing to a conversation. He was putting multiple words together in proper syntax, and *they* sounded beautiful.

Undaunted by our experience, I made a telephone call to Kutztown University. I spoke to a professor in the music department who recommended I meet with a recent graduate. Tara and Justin hit it off from the first lesson. Instantly, Tara was amazed as Justin repeated sounds she called "vocal-ease." As she described it, he went through them "like a hot knife through butter." Justin naturally imitated everything Tara sang. Although he was young and his voice had not yet changed, Tara was so curious she just *had* to test the range of his voice. He followed her keyboard perfectly through three octaves. She taught him songs in foreign languages. Tara realized that Justin practiced more often by listening than by actually singing, so she made tapes for him. He would listen to them repeatedly and occasionally sing along. Sometimes he would sing one line from the middle of a song over and over again. Jill and I thought he was perseverating. Tara felt he was practicing and explained that she often told her students to do exactly that, but they rarely listened to her advice. I asked her if I was just another "stage" parent who thought his child had a great singing voice. Tara looked at me with the straightest face and said, "Let me tell you, if I had his ability, I would *not* be teaching voice lessons."

As his voice began to change, Justin outgrew Tara. She could not sing in his deeper tone and he could not imitate her at the higher octaves. I called Kutztown University for another recommendation. This time, after explaining the situation to Dr. Williams, the head of the department, he asked if I would allow *him* to teach Justin. At Justin's first lesson, the tutor went through some vocal-ease, which Justin already knew. Dr. Williams complimented Justin's former teacher saying, "Someone taught him well."

Dr. Williams expanded Justin's repertoire to include songs in foreign languages. One thing I *really* like about Dr. Williams is that he treats Justin like he would any other student. He sits and explains to Justin everything about a song—from the meaning of the words, to the reason why there is a pause at a particular place.

Jill and I have always known what we wanted for Justin. We wanted him to play the violin and sing with his peers, to socialize, and get physical exercise. To supplement the exercise, we became involved with Special Olympics. They had a basketball team and accepted all levels of ability. We liked the idea of a team sport. This would give him exercise and socialization together. Justin liked playing basketball and enjoyed being with the members of the team, but did not get the concept of the game. He does not have a competitive bone in his body. When playing against another team, Justin would just as soon give the ball away. Justin's introduction to Special Olympics came with an added bonus—the coach heard Justin singing to himself and asked if he would like to sing the national anthem at the opening ceremony of the Eastern County Special Olympics.

The first time Justin sang at this annual event, organizers had to rip the microphone from his hands, as he thought the applause meant the crowd wanted him to sing another song. At our request, Justin was not asked to sing every year. Some years he did not sing, and other years, he sang with a group. Once, Justin was asked to sing "God Bless America." In 2001, he was invited to perform the national anthem solo. Ever the supportive father, I stood a few feet from my son as he began, "Oh say, can you see ..." He kept looking over at me with a devious grin. You need to understand that if Justin were a typical child, he would be the class prankster. I do know Justin, so I knew he was up to something. I just had no idea what it was. While he sang, I pleaded with him, "Whatever you are planning to do, do not do it." I repeated this admonition several times, and Justin just kept grinning. Then, it happened. We all know the part in the national anthem where we are supposed to hit that high note on "free," and we have all heard many voices crack while reaching for it. Well, Justin decided it would be comical to miss the high note on purpose. I was furious! Yes, I will admit it was funny, but I did not like 4,000 fans thinking he could not reach that note.

Justin, at times, has a wonderful sense of humor. Like any parent, I also want him to know that everything has its time and place. The results Jill and I are looking for are different than what other parents of children who perform as well as Justin may be looking for. Many parents want people to see that their children perform *better* than everyone else's does. *We* want everyone to see that our child is *just* like everyone else's child. He is a person first and foremost, and should not be defined by a diagnosis. Autism is what he *has*, not who he is.

This year, we have included orchestra and chorus in Justin's Individual Educational Plan, yet we *still* had to convince the teachers that Justin was a valuable asset. Once the teachers heard Justin play and sing, they welcomed him warmly. Justin is no longer "officially" in music therapy, but I happen to disagree. I believe the study of music to be therapeutic for *all* human beings. I do not think anyone denies the soothing nature of some styles of music. I do not think anyone would disagree that playing an instrument, any instrument, releases tension. Studies have shown that students who study music fare better in mathematics than students who do not. In my opinion, these are qualities found in therapy.

Justin, Jill, and I feel that playing the violin has allowed Justin to excel in an area in which the playing field has been leveled. It has earned him the respect of his peers. It has demonstrated that students with special needs can succeed.

When Justin started playing the violin in grade school there were more than 100 students in orchestra. Our daughter, Alexandra, is three years younger than Justin is. She attends a different school, where every student in her grade is in the orchestra. Students are expected to participate in music, just as they would math and language arts. Justin is now in high school and, sadly, the orchestra has only about 30 students.

I do not have a musical note in my body; however, I have always been active in sports. I have always contended that playing a team sport teaches people about teamwork and cooperation, competition, and fair play. It teaches respect for oneself and one's competitor, about hard work, success, and failure. Playing sports, I have argued, teaches people about life. These same arguments can and should be used to promote the study of orchestra, chorus, band, and other fine arts subjects. Speaking for all students, I believe that music, more than sports, is an area where appropriate inclusion benefits all students.

Due to his success in music therapy, music lessons, violin lessons, and voice lessons, Jill and I have seen Justin's peers approach him after a concert and congratulate him on a job well done. We have seen these children interact with him, just as they would any other child. Justin feels accepted because he is accepted as a valued member of the "group." Jill and I often comment that Justin's peers are getting as much out of Justin's music therapy as *he* is. The world will ultimately have to interact with people like Justin, and Justin will have to live in this world. What better place to start learning than in school!

This article first appeared in the Fall 2003 issue of the Arizona Music News. *Reprinted by permission.*

Hearing Impairments: An Alert for All Music Educators

Lyn E. Schraer-Joiner

As educators, our primary goal is to meet our students' educational needs regardless of their varying backgrounds, skills, and physiological conditions. At times, however, our strenuous and overloaded schedules can cause us to look at our students as myriad faces rather than as individuals. As a result, we may fail to recognize signs which can be a deterrent to their musical experiences. For example, hearing loss may discourage them from joining an ensemble, volunteering to play the bass xylophone in a general music class, or simply communicating in musical ways.

Terms to Know

To understand how music learning is possible for children with hearing loss, educators should be familiar with the terminology, processes, and misconceptions commonly associated with hearing loss. Often, the assumption is made that people with hearing impairments are incapable of perceiving any sound and thus lack the ability to learn, perceive, and enjoy music (Campbell, 1995, p. 345). Many individuals, however, possess residual audition, the hearing that remains after the onset of a loss, therefore retaining some capacity to hear musical sound and respond to and perform music.

Differences between the terms "hearing impaired," "hard of hearing," and "deafness" are often either unknown or misunderstood. An impairment is any loss of physiological or psychological structure or function considered normal for human beings (Marschark, 1997, p.7). The terms "hard of hearing" and "deaf" are both defined by the law PL94142 (Atterbury, 1990, p. 104). The phrase "hard of hearing," commonly used when describing hearing loss, refers to a permanent or fluctuating hearing impairment, which adversely affects a child's educational performance (p. 104). A child classified as "hard of hearing" can perceive a sufficient amount of sound enabling them to understand speech, and can communicate in a manner similar to that of a hearing child (Campbell, 1995, p. 345). The term "deafness," however, is defined as a hearing impairment so severe that the child cannot process linguistic information without amplification (Atterbury, 1990, p. 104). The meaning of this term changes when utilized with either a capital "D" or lower case 'd." For example, the word Deaf is used as an adjective, and refers to a group of people totally incapable of receiving or perceiving sound. This group views themselves as a community bound together by a common culture and language, which is generally American Sign Language (ASL). The word deaf is a general term associated with the causes and subsequent severity of hearing loss and whether the hearing mechanism can be used for communication purposes (Marschark, 1997, p. 6). Distinctions such as these have received such focus because people who are deaf are often described in medical terms rather than as a people with rich cultural traditions (p. 6).

The Hearing Process

Intensity (the physical property of loudness) ranges associated with hearing loss are defined in terms of the extent that ordinary speech must be magnified in order to be heard (Birkenshaw-Fleming, 1993, p. 71). According to Marschark (1997) the following decibel levels represent the limit of potential hearing in a specific frequency range (Marschark, 1997, p. 29). For example, hearing is considered normal with losses up to 25 decibels (dB); mild hearing loss, 26–40 dB; moderate hearing loss, 41–55 dB; moderately severe hearing loss, 56–70 dB; severe hearing loss, 71–90 dB; and profound loss, greater than 90 dB (p. 29). In comparison, total deafness is the inability to perceive any sound, regardless of amplification. Children with mild hearing losses can comprehend conversation from a distance of three to five feet and tend to become confused in group situations. They also rely upon speech reading. Children with moderate hearing losses can understand loud conversations and tend to have impaired language and speech comprehension. Severely deafened children may hear loud sounds up to one foot from the ear and can identify some environmental sound as well. However, they have difficulty with speech and language skill development and rely heavily upon visual cues as a result. Profoundly deafened children may be able to perceive some loud sounds but primarily sense vibration. They will also have difficulty with speech and language skill development and also rely upon visual cuing (Campbell, 1995, p. 347).

Types of Loss

Hearing loss may be caused by damage or deterioration to any part of the hearing mechanism before, during, or after birth. The age at which hearing loss occurs may strongly influence a child's development and communication skills. A child with a congenital hearing loss, which is acquired during fetal development, is at a greater risk for delays in music and oral language development than a child who acquires a hearing loss after a period of normal auditory experience. Conductive hearing losses result from damage to the ear drum or bones of the middle ear and are generally caused by accidents, ear infections, diseases, or can be congenital. Such defects restrict the transmission of vibrations through the middle ear—thus affecting one's hearing acuity. Sensorineural losses generally have an effect on perception of the clarity of sound and can be caused by damage to or deterioration of the nerve fibers within the inner ear or the auditory nerve. Losses of this type can be either congenital or acquired and can lead to the absence of hearing at specific or all frequency levels (Nocera, 1979, p. 241). Other potential causes of sensorineural hearing loss include prolonged exposure to sustained noise levels of approximately 85 dB or greater, excessive intake of medication such as aspirin and some antibiotics and chronic ear infections which have spread from the middle to the inner ear (Atterbury, 1990, p. 106).

Symptoms of Hearing Loss

Signs that a teacher may observe to identify a hearing loss include a student's failure to perceive or respond to environmental sounds (especially startling sounds), the misinterpretation of spoken language, behavioral abnormalities, or discharge from the ears. Hearing losses also are likely if a child shows difficulty in discriminating environmental sounds, constantly increases the loudness of the radio or television, often asks people to repeat speech, or says "what?" frequently when in conversation. Other indications that a student may have a hearing loss include impaired speech or speech irregularities, a limited vocabulary, a shortened attention span, unexplained discipline problems, or easily provoked frustration. If hearing loss is suspected, music educators should review, with appropriate consent, the student's records, consult the school nurse and other teachers, and/or contact the child's parents in order to determine if the child's family is aware of hearing problems or has a history of hearing loss. If the music educator suspects a hearing loss, this concern should be brought to the attention of the classroom teacher or appropriate school staff member so that a hearing test can be arranged according to school policies.

What Do I Need to Know for the Enhancement of Those with Hearing Loss?

In order to provide an appropriate learning environment for students with hearing loss, the music educator should investigate the student's history and resolutions to hearing problems that may already be employed. These include (a) communication with classroom teachers, the school nurse, and school counselors; (b) the amplification equipment used by hard of hearing students; (c) procedures being used to teach the students in their other classes; (d) classroom adaptations to accommodate the handicapped; and (e) alternative forms of communication, including both Cued Speech which supports spoken language with a set of sound-related hand shapes or Signed English which combines English grammar with the signs of American Sign Language (Campbell, 1995, p. 347).

The music educator has a professional obligation to maintain communication with classroom teachers, the school nurse, and school counselors so that the student's progress can be monitored and program goals and approaches changed as needed. Amplification instruments such as hearing aids, and hearing aids with a microphone and "FM boot," also identified as "auditory training," are devices that children with hearing loss may use effectively. Music teachers should become familiar with any enhancement devices that their students use or can obtain, while also recognizing the fact that musical sounds will be made louder by amplification devices, in many cases resulting in the distortion of sound quality and pitch range (Beer, 1980, p. 61). Distortions originating from ambient classroom noise or various rhythm and melody instruments should be discussed with these students for clarification and explanation of the student's perceptions of these sounds. Students may, as a result of these distortions, need to decrease the output of their hearing aids in group singing or instrumental activities. Optimal levels of loudness should be determined on the basis of teacher-student interaction (Campbell, 1995, p. 348).

To provide equality in education for children with hearing loss, the music educator must also be familiar with the methods and procedures being used to teach those children in their other classes. Oral communication approaches place emphasis upon auditory, visual, and tactile modes of communication. One example is auditory learning, a method which focuses on instructing the student to listen to actual sounds, comprehension through careful attention to the speaker's face, and speech reading. The reader who wishes to pursue the details showing applications of these areas may consult books such as *Raising and Educating a Deaf Child: A Comprehensive Guide to the Choices, Controversies, and Decisions Faced by Parents and Educators* by Marc Marschark and *Music in Childhood: From Preschool through the Elementary Grades* by Patricia Shehan Campbell and Carol

Scott-Kassner.

Assuming the music teacher has made a thorough attempt to meet the needs of all the students in the music classroom, adaptations in normal classroom procedure may still be required for hard of hearing and deaf students. Music educators should consider the following suggestions (Campbell, 1995, p. 347):

1. Seat the child at the front of the room making sure the light falls on the face of the teacher, speaker, or performer.
2. Seat the child next to the sound source (piano, drum, or speaker).
3. Use pantomime, facial expressions, or body language in order to help communicate.
4. Face the child when speaking directly to him or her.
5. Speak clearly, making sure to articulate each word.
6. Do not speak quickly.
7. Do not shout or raise the level of your voice.
8. Visually cue the child first if you are going to ask a question.

Other forms of visual communication include the use of icons, pictures, charts, overheads, and printed class notes which can all be utilized to emphasize important information including page numbers for songs and words representing key concepts (Beer, 1980, p. 62).

Equal Opportunities Are Key

According to Darrow (1990), a classroom is truly integrated only if the teacher makes an effort to include special students instead of merely accommodating them (Darrow, 1990, p. 36). To do this, Darrow suggests implementing a multilevel and, whenever possible, a multisensory approach. This will not only be of benefit to the hearing impaired students but the normal hearing students as well. The multilevel approach will assist in enabling all students to participate and be successful, as opposed to a select few (p. 37). Due to the fact that children with profound loss will be unable to hear music, the music educator may consider having them touch and feel the vibration of instruments being utilized such as the soundboard of a piano, the body of a guitar, or side of a drum. If the class focus is centered upon pitch discrimination or instrument playing activities, music teachers can provide hard of hearing or deaf children with instruments in which the vibration can be felt with the hand, such as rhythm sticks or wood block (Beer, 1980, p. 62). Meter and rhythm can be approached by having students tap patterns on their desks or other sound-conducting surfaces with their hands. Music educators may also consider placing stereo speakers or instruments such as a piano or xylophone on a wooden floor or platform as another way to enhance the resonance of the sound production—thus acoustically amplifying the sounds produced. In such situations, hard of hearing or deaf children should be encouraged to participate without shoes so that they can feel the vibrations through their feet (Campbell, 1995, p. 348). Music with very strong beats and driving rhythms is appropriate for such activities.

Other suggestions facilitating the integration of exceptional children into the music lesson include use of teachers' aides to accompany special students to music class, assignment of classroom "buddies" and peer tutors to assist students who need specialized attention, and input from special education teachers in the development of classroom resources and materials (Darrow, 1990, p.37). The music classroom environment can also serve a significant role in promoting an acceptance and understanding of hearing impairments, thus helping to diminish misconceptions of teachers and students and reducing social barriers associated with hearing loss. Lessons which include signing songs or performing folk songs such as "I Bought Me a Cat" or "Mr. Frog Went A'Courtin'" in which the children have the opportunity to assume the parts of various animals such as the frog, mouse, or snake can facilitate positive interactions which will benefit all children involved (Walczyk, 1993, p. 42).

Music Educators Never Fear: Your Resources Are Here.

Music educators who have not been trained to educate exceptional children need not feel ineffective when faced with this responsibility, as a wealth of resources are available. Immediate resources, as previously mentioned, include the special education or classroom teacher who can provide an extensive background about the hearing impaired student, approaches for teaching, methods of communication, and hearing equipment. The child's Individual Education Plan (IEP) is also a resource which will provide a comprehensive background regarding the educational goals and objectives for that child. Other sources include written statements by the classroom teacher of the child's current achievement and educational level, educational services the child may be receiving such as physical or occupational therapy, mainstream programs, and evaluation procedures which will help the music teacher attain specified goals. Physical or occupational therapists also can provide information regarding students' limitations and areas of strength.

Once the music teacher has an understanding of the student's capabilities, he or she can determine how to effectively approach the child. The music supervisor and other music educators also can be of assistance by sharing similar experiences, effective lessons, and activities for the successful inclusion of the hard of hearing or deaf child. Organizations such as the American Association for Music Therapy (AAMT), the North Carolina Music Educators Association (NCMEA), and MENC: The National Association for Music Education also can be valuable resources for instructional materials and resources for children with hearing losses. These organizations often provide specific journal or magazine articles focusing on hearing impairments and also suggest resource people who have completed research in these areas.

Additional resources such as the Council for Exceptional Children (CEC), the Alexander Graham Bell Association for the Deaf, and the National Association of the Deaf (NAD) are available to aid the music educator and can be found on the Project Reach Web site located at http://www.uncg.edu/~leschrae/ Project_reach _cover.html (Schraer-Joiner, 2000).

Conclusions

Although hearing loss can limit musical capacity, hearing impaired children are able to respond to musical stimuli and should be offered the same opportunities as their peers. Music deserves a place in the curriculum of the deaf and hard of hearing, just as all children deserve the right to experience the different facets of their cultural heritage and to develop their aural, artistic, aesthetic, and musical senses to the best of their abilities. If approached properly and planned so that the education of the normal hearing children is not sacrificed, the music classroom can provide wonderful experiences for children with hearing losses, including further development of perceptual skills, socialization, and musical understanding. Although this planning will undoubtedly require assistance and some training for the music educator, children with hearing losses can and should utilize their residual audition to participate with their classmates in singing, listening, playing, moving, and creating music (Marschark, 1997, p. 194). All students should be allowed to embrace music as a special part of their lives and music teachers must be prepared to provide appropriate musical experiences.

References

Atterbury, B. (1990). *Mainstreaming exceptional children.* New Jersey: Prentice Hall.

Birkenshaw-Fleming, L. (1993). *Music for all: Teaching music to people with special needs.* Canada: Gordon V. Thompson Music.

Campbell, P & Scott-Kassner, C. (1995). *Music in childhood: From preschool through the elementary grades.* New York: Schirmer Books.

Darrow, A. A. (1985). Music for the deaf. *Music Educators Journal,* 71(6), 33–35.

Darrow, A. A. (1987). The arts of sign and song. *Music Educators Journal,* 74(1), 33–35.

Darrow, A. A. (1990). Beyond mainstreaming: Dealing with diversity. *Music Educators Journal,* 76(8), 36–43.

Darrow, A. A. (1990). The role of hearing in understanding music. *Music Educators Journal,* 77(4), 24–27.

Darrow, A. A. & Gfellar, K. (1991). A study of public school music programs mainstreaming hearing impaired students. *Journal of Music Therapy,* 28, 22–31.

Fahey, J. & Birkenshaw, L. (1972). Bypassing the ear: The perception of music by feeling and touch. *Music Educators Journal,* 58(8), 44–49.

Graham, R. & Beer, A. (1980). *A handbook for mainstreaming: Teaching music to the exceptional child.* New Jersey: Prentice Hall.

Madsen, C. & Mears, W. (1965). The effect of sound upon the tactile threshold of deaf subjects. *Journal of Music Therapy,* 2, 64–68.

Marschark, M. (1997). *Raising and educating a deaf child.* New York: Oxford University Press.

Martin, F & Clark, J. (1996). *Hearing care for children.* Boston: Allyn and Bacon.

Morgan, A. (1987). Causes and treatment of hearing loss in children, In Martin, F. ed. *Hearing disorders in children: Pediatric audiology.* Austin: Pro-Ed, Inc.

Nocera, S. (1979). *Reaching the special learner through music.* New Jersey: Silver Burdett Company.

Schraer-Joiner, L. (2000). Project reach [Online]. Available: http://www.uncg.edu/~leschrae/Project_reach_cover.html.

Shannon, R. (1989). The psychophysics of cochlear implant stimulation, in Owens, E. & Kessler, D. eds. *Cochlear implants in young deaf children*. Boston: College Hill Press.

Walczyk, E. (1993). Music instruction and the hearing impaired. *Music Educators Journal*, 80(1), 42–44.

This article first appeared in the Winter 2003 issue of the North Carolina Music Educator. *Reprinted by permission.*

Teaching Music to Sighted and Visually-Impaired Students

Wayne R. Siligo

The following observations are a result of thirty years of teaching music in public and private music schools and studios. During the past eighteen years I have been the director of music education at the California School for the Blind (CSB). I am a graduate of California State University at Hayward, and received my special-education training in the graduate program at San Francisco State University, maintaining a 4.0 grade-point average. I am blind as a result of a progressive retinal disease identified in my early teens. I was classically trained as an operatic tenor and enjoyed a great deal of early success, winning several competitions and appearing with both the San Francisco and San Jose Symphony Orchestras. As my vision failed, I soon discovered that the opportunities for the blind in the professional classical performance field were minimal. I always had an interest in jazz and show music. So, during my late twenties I turned to playing guitar and singing in clubs and resort hotels, while continuing my first passion—teaching. In January 1999, I celebrated my fifteenth consecutive year of playing guitar, saxophone, and piano at the same five-star French restaurant near Mission San Jose, California. In November 1996, the students of our music program at CSB and I were honored to appear on the second segment of a Fox Network news special broadcast from Jack London Square in Oakland, California on KTVU.

During the last few years, rarely a week has passed that I have not received a telephone call from a public or private music teacher or concerned parent who was requesting information or advice about teaching a blind or visually impaired child or adult. Many of the questions they have asked I address below, and I will be glad to share information and answer questions anyone might have in the future. Most of the topics discussed below are also applicable to the teaching of sighted students.

After years of teaching vocal and instrumental music, I am solidly convinced that students' early progress is not always an indication of their future success. This early unpredictability results from a variety of reasons, for example students' lack of familiarity with new or first instruments, and/or their early lack of confidence. One factor, often overlooked, is the need for good student/teacher compatibility and rapport. It is not unusual for new students to be uneasy and find it difficult to absorb the material being taught, not only because of being unsure about their own abilities, but also perhaps because of feeling somewhat intimidated by the teacher's performance level and professional manner, especially during one-to-one individual instruction. It is important that teachers make students comfortable and at ease as soon as possible. This will help in opening up the lines of communication, which will then allow the teacher to begin the learning process easily. I have found that showing a genuine interest in the student's outside hobbies and leisure activities is a comfortable point of conversation to use in beginning this process. Showing an interest in, and a knowledge of, a new student's musical tastes, as well as favorite performing groups and artists, is also a means to open up a comfortable dialogue and establish rapport. Though our own tastes in styles of music may differ by 180 degrees from those of our younger pupils, the fact that we are aware of their generation's music quickly begins to build a rapport between teacher and student.

Evaluation is one of the primary factors in the overall effectiveness of teaching music skills and techniques. The teacher must assess and identify students' strong and weak musical attributes, and not expect them to perform or master skills that they are physiologically or developmentally incapable of at a particular stage of their musical developments. This is especially true when dealing with transfer students. Setting unrealistic goals and objectives for new students can erect unwanted barriers to their chances of success and cause negative effects to their self-esteem and confidence. This is especially important when teaching students with disabilities. Sadly, not all parents of disabled children are always realistic concerning their children's musical abilities and futures. These children should be given the freedom and dignity of progressing at their own level of proficiency without the added burden of unrealistic expectations. Reality is sometimes cruel, but not nearly as cruel as those who give disabled students false hopes and unrealistic expectations. These students are often told that they can do anything they desire, in spite of their disabilities. The same success factors that should be accounted for in the cases of students who are able-bodied also should be accounted for in the cases of students with disabilities: opportunity, physical dexterity, coordination, a skilled and devoted teacher, and, of course, aptitude for music. No one likes to fail—this is a known trait of human behavior—so to promise, expect, or demand more than a student can produce at any given time is not only counterproductive in terms of the teacher's goals, but is also a sure-fire guarantee of the student's failure and will probably result in loss of interest and desire. To challenge and demand excellence is one thing, but to set up failure from lack of proper evaluation and sensitivity is entirely another matter.

Another point related to the importance of evaluation is that it is always a difficult task to inform a parent or guardian of a transferred student that the instrument his or her child has been struggling to play, with little or no success (and often it was purchased at great expense), is not at all suitable for the student because of fine motor or other physical restrictions. Decisions as to the future musical direction and type of instrument to which the beginning student is best suited should be accomplished only after an extended period of trial and observation, always keeping in mind the student's wishes. Though the student may be perfectly suited to play the instrument we may have selected, its sound may not be appealing to the new player. The teacher should ask these questions: Is the instrument I have selected for this student the one that is most needed in my program, or is it the one that is most suited to the student's future leisure use? Will it give the student the most pleasure and musical satisfaction? Compassion and tact must be used when discussing a student's limitations, and we should always have an alternate suggestion or recommendation for the new student, whatever his or her physical limitations might be. To a child with limited skills, playing the woodblock in an ensemble can be just as joyful and rewarding as blowing an awesome solo would be for a gifted, advanced student.

Assumption is one of the pitfalls that all teachers experience at some point, especially when teaching students who have had prior instruction. It is important from the very first lesson that we be aware of a student's ability to grasp conceptual ideas and abstract verbal models of rhythmic figures, e.g., "one a fun duh, two a fun duh, three a fun duh" to represent the sound of sixteenth notes, or "one triplet, two triplet, three triplet" to represent the sound of eighth-note triplets, etc. We should not assume that the new student understands this technique and order of verbalizing rhythm, or any other abstract technique, for that matter. Facts and concepts that may seem simplistic to teachers still need to be carefully explained. We must keep our explanations and definitions short, with simple vocabulary. Often, beginning students are lost when a teacher dwells too much on pedantic details of theory and terminology rather than on the crux of music itself—melody and rhythm. It is my firm belief that every beginning student should be taught simple melodies as soon as possible, even by ear for those who possess the aural capability to do do so. This gives beginning players confidence and immediately makes their instruments less intimidating to them. It also gives them a sense of accomplishment from the very start of their musical journeys. The teacher should never lose sight of the often-forgotten fact that music notation is only a means to an end. The sound of the music and the timbres of the different instruments are what draw students to take lessons in the first place.

It is imperative that the teacher explain to new students that an interesting and somewhat disturbing phenomenon will more than likely take place. Many of their closest friends, and relatives as well, may tease and ridicule them, and often will not be tolerant of the rather annoying sounds of their efforts, especially if they are playing any of the horns or any member of the string family. New students should be helped to understand that this is due to a variety of reasons, for instance, envy or jealousy of their talents or of the attention they are receiving from the teacher and from other friends who appreciate their new challenge and skill. A good part of the complaining will be due to the listeners' lack of tolerance for repetitious sound and to their inability to project ahead and imagine what the new student will sound like in a few months' time.

For new singers or instrumentalists to progress at their most efficient rates, it is imperative that the teacher instruct them in how to practice. As simplistic as this may sound, it is an acquired skill, and quite often new students do not have a clue as to how to organize the content of their practice time. For many, it is common in most facets of our lives to lean toward the things we do the best and shy away from those that we find difficult or foreign. This certainly applies as we learn music skills and techniques. It is much easier to play and enjoy the pieces and skills we have mastered and of which we are confident, rather than those we find too technical or demanding. However, the process of musical growth ceases whenever more challenging material is not introduced and mastered. So it is a continuously important task for the teacher to find music for students that is not only enjoyable to play, but also requires use of the musical skills and techniques currently being emphasized. Students should be taught to organize their practice time in order to maximize its use. This is not always an easy process. By their nature, some students are more organized than others and blessed with a gift for staying on task. A most important task before practice begins is for the new student and his or her parents to find not only a time during the day, but also a location or room, that will afford the student the best opportunity to practice without being disturbed by, or disturbing, others in the family. Obviously, this will eliminate the occurrence of the complaining phenomenon mentioned earlier.

The following practice order has had a fairly good track record for me in the past: In the first section of the practice period, the student should concentrate on long tones and breath-control exercises when playing the horns or woodwinds. This also accomplishes the process of warming-up the embouchure and helps develop better tone quality. Bowing and finger vibrato should be practiced during this time on the stringed instruments. Next, the scales, inversions, and arpeggios that are presently being studied, as well as mechanical fingering and digital techniques unique to the student's instrument should be practiced with enough repetitions to insure the process of digital memory and effect a slight increase in overall speed. The content of this section would be structured by the teacher.

The second, or middle, section of the practice period should be devoted to the practice of whatever pieces, classical or popular, that are currently being studied, as well as any other performance material that needs attention. This is also a good time to practice ensemble parts if the teacher allows the student to take the individual, notated parts home. The student should be encouraged to practice fragments of the pieces being learned and to spend extra time on the sections that are proving to be particularly difficult. This is a method of practicing that allows the student to learn the pieces from the inside out, so to speak. Braille music readers learn in exactly this manner, gradually adding measures at each practice session. (Obviously, blind students cannot perform and read braille music at the same time, except while sight-singing or while playing the few instruments that are fingered with only one hand.) Using the order I have suggested here for practice sessions allows students to work on tedious and more repetitious material at the beginning of each session, while they are still fresh and eager to practice.

The third, and last section of the practice period should consist of whatever the student wants to play or work on, whether or not it applies to what the teacher has been emphasizing. The content of this section could include improvising, as well as the exploration of existing pieces new to the student, either by ear (including auding—learning pieces from prerecorded audio material) or by using whatever written music medium is applicable for the student. If a blind or visually impaired student is in your program, his or her ensemble parts and lesson material can be recorded on tape. Often, this recording can be done by another more advanced student for extra credit. If the music student is a braille music reader, ensemble parts and solos can be transcribed in braille by a certified Braille Music Transcriber. The braille music contact person with the California Transcribers and Educators of the Visually Handicapped is Richard Taesch (telephone 818-767-6554). In the past, this was a time-consuming and costly process, but with modern electronic tools and computers it is now much more efficient and less costly. Ambitious sighted teachers who want to learn to transcribe print music to braille music themselves can do so by purchasing a Braille Transcribers manual (available both in print and braille) from the American Printing House for the Blind Inc. (1839 Frankfort Ave., P.O. 6085, Louisville, KY 40206-0085; telephone 502-895-2405). The Duxbury Braille Transcription software program allows a sighted user to enter six-dot music or literary Braille cells into a computer. From the computer, information is printed into paper Braille on a Braille embosser or printer. Quite often, Braille embossers are found in the special education resource rooms of public schools.

For those students who are learning the skill of auding, the teacher must be sure that the tape player being used is playing on pitch. If not, a player with a pitch control would be a great asset.

These are available from the American Printing House for the Blind in Louisville, Kentucky. Aiwa and Sony Corporations also manufacture tape players that have pitch controls and are affordable. At the end of the practice session, the player could also spend some time just enjoying the playing of old pieces that he or she might wish to review. Many of my more advanced students like to use this time to improve their reading skills, from either print or Braille. Jazz players also need to put aside time for improvising to recorded background chord changes played by, or provided by, the teacher, or along with prerecorded jazz improvisation tapes or compact discs, e.g., the Jamey Aebersold series for horn players, and Frank Semaris's *Jazz Piano* series for piano and keyboard students. The series by Frank Semaris is also a fine source for modern jazz-keyboard voicings. To acquire his series, Frank can be reached at Chabot College in Hayward, California. There is a new jazz-improvisation CD titled *The Standard of Excellence Jazz Ensemble Method*, which is available from Neil Kjos Music Co. (4380 Jutland Drive, San Diego, CA 92117). It is intended mainly for horn players, but I find it useful for all solo instruments, and many diverse styles of jazz and blues are featured. Jazz students who use such prerecorded tapes and CDs should also jam or rehearse with other students, preferably with those who are slightly more advanced.

Since many blind music students have the gift of perfect pitch, I have always found it less confusing and far more practical to use concert pitch while teaching them their fingerings and musical parts. Those teachers who are familiar with the Perkins Brailler can use the following techniques I have developed: Relate the finger positions of the horns to the Brailler. The first, second, and third fingers of the left hand, and the first, second, and third fingers of the right hand, form the fingering for the concert pitch F on the alto saxophone and the concert pitch C on the tenor saxophone. The same fingering on the Brailler forms the braille symbol for the word "for." The fingering that forms the Braille symbol for the letter R also forms the fingering for the concert pitch A on the alto saxophone and the concert pitch E on the tenor saxophone. By means of similar comparisons, this technique can be transferred easily to other instruments, e.g., clarinet, flute, and valved horns.

Another observation I have made is that students do consistently better when they are made accountable for practice time. This can be accomplished easily with the use of three-by-five-inch index cards. Have the student's parents or caregiver initial and date each day the student practices. This technique is, of course, more appropriate for younger students, but is not out of the question for older players who need to be motivated to stay on task or who enjoy the reassurance that the teacher knows that they have practiced.

The part of the curriculum that is the most rewarding and the most important to the long-term success of music students is that of concentrated ear-training. Through the years I have seen far too many players tied to the security and boundaries of the printed pages of the music. For some players, I believe this process stifles interpretation and creativity. I have observed that many of these same players seldom show an interest in composition and quite often do not improvise well. Though some may disagree, I believe that print and braille music notation are not merely vehicles to recreate musical sound, but are an important means for us to assimilate and store music, and then draw from the composer's creativity, thus making the music an integral addition to our own creative talents and skills. Along with ear-training, the skill of memorizing must be taught and emphasized from the earliest time the student begins to learn solo performance material. This applies to both recitals and school concerts. Of course, this practice would not usually apply to large-ensemble groups of sighted players using print music arrangements or jazz charts. The art of memorizing, however, is a learned skill, and becomes more effective and less difficult with time and repetition. Though for some students it may be difficult or almost impossible at first, memorizing forces or encourages the receptive centers and pathways of the brain to organize the musical sounds and phrases heard, enabling the development of more and more sensitivity to tonal and melodic relationships. Though both are abstract, I believe ear-training and memorizing are simultaneously supportive. I am convinced that memorizing, through repetition, automatically helps the student develop what I term "active listening" skills, along with better overall tonal memory. The process of memorizing, when coupled with intensive ear-training (consisting of harmonic voicing and chordal recognition, combined with intervallic familiarity and a good background in the recognition and use of all scale forms, in both major and minor tonal centers), is the foundation for becoming not only a literate, but also a complete and articulate, musician. I have seen this demonstrated in hundreds of students of all levels, whether learning-challenged or not. Even accomplished players who exclusively use print music at all times must be convinced that it is never too late to begin ear-training. To a serious musician, having an untrained ear is about as useful as a Mark 6 tenor saxophone without a reed. I distinctly remember attending a formal birthday party where a pianist had been hired to play background music. He played quite well, using print music the entire time, but when the time came to present the cake, the pianist was unable to play even a simple chordal accompaniment for the singing of "Happy Birthday to You," because he did not have printed music for the song. A little harmonic ear-training would have saved him a from an embarrassing moment.

Students who decide they want to learn to play a musical instrument but who do not possess a great amount of natural music ability are not at all unusual. Like everyone else, they deserve to be allowed the joy and leisure activity of participating in a music program by learning to play instruments whose technical levels of mastery match their physical skills and coordination. These students are the very ones who can be helped the most by being nurtured musically in the program of an experienced and assessment-minded teacher. These same students are those who often do well in a structured, print-music environment, without a great deal of emphasis on ear-training or memorizing. Reading and playing music is a wonderful means of meeting their needs for creative activity and also adds to their self-esteem. As teachers, we must not forget that this last group of students mentioned deserve every bit as much of our effort and energy as those who possess the talent to later become performing musicians at a professional level.

Simply stated, I believe it is not only the task, but also the obligation, of the music teacher and mentor to search for and provide the best and most fulfilling music curriculum and program to ensure students' success and growth. We must always remember that each new and excited musician is trusting the development of his or her skills and aspirations to our patience, adaptability, and understanding.

This article first appeared in the Fall 1999 issue of the Colorado Music Educator. *Reprinted by permission.*

Loud, Louder, Loudest: Teaching the Dynamics of Life

Elise S. Sobol

For the young, severely emotionally disturbed student who knows conflict, controversy, and violence, teaching soft, softer, and softest is so necessary for the development of a healthier and socially positive well-being. Asking severely disturbed individuals to play softly on the hand drums or drumset, maracas, or tambourines will so often times draw a blank response. Cognitively these students just haven't experienced soft. In their world of noise, students know screaming and yelling, agitation and anxiety, high amplification with pulsating, earth shattering motion and movement. Silence is not golden. Silence is fraught with the fears of abandonment and rejection. Silence is cold, not safely filled with feelings of attachment, warmth, comfort, or beauty.

A classroom music teacher is gifted in being able to educate the whole child—his heart, his mind, and his body. Music can provide the forum to guide and enrich a student's life, making him capable of expressing the dynamics of life from softest to the loudest.

How can we break through the loud, hardened violent skin of a severely emotionally damaged young student? This tough skin has developed in the student as a protection against more hurt. How can we, in a nonthreatening way, help find points of calm, beauty, and safety for these students in music class?

Ed Young in *Voices of the Heart* (Scholastic Press, New York, 1997) invites all children, young and old, to explore the many voices from our heart. The virtuous heart, the shameful heart, the understanding heart, the forgiving heart, the joyful heart, the sorrowful heart, the respectful heart, the rude heart, the contented heart, the despairing heart, the lazy heart, the able heart, the graceful heart, the forgetful heart, the resentful heart, the constant heart, the aspiring heart, the frightened heart, the merciful heart, the tolerant heart, the angry heart, the silenced heart, the evil heart, the doubtful heart, and the loyal heart. Mr. Young is an artist, he expresses his thoughts through Chinese characters and visual collage. As musicians we can teach these thoughts through the language of music notation and sound. We can broaden the lives of our students by exposing them to pleasant sound experiences.

What are our soft and pleasant sound experiences that we can bring to the attention of our students?

Let's start with the magical sounds in nature. Tranquil ocean waves offer a sea of tranquillity. Like the fetus in the womb, the protecting waters envelop and bring nourishment to the new life. There is a feeling of safety. Anger and aggression need not be displayed. The winds whistle, the brooks gurgle, the trees sigh, the horses neigh, the cats purr, the frogs croak, and little lambs baa. Quiet little musicians can be found in the tall summer grass waving in the breeze. There are fiddling crickets, buzzing bees, chattering squirrels, squeaking mice, and trilling toads. All these are nice sounds, good sounds, pleasant to our ears. These are sounds we should teach our students whether through a walk in the woods or arboretum or on wonderful sound records that bring nature to our ears. Examples of other nonthreatening sounds include those of songbirds—each uniquely expressing their special needs through an ability to sing in musical patterns. Ornithologists have developed memory phrases for us to learn to recognize common songbirds. The red cardinal sings, "hurry home-hurry home" while the bluebird says, "churr-cheerful charmer." The robin's song will remind us to "cheerup-cheerily-cheerup, cheerup, cheerup."

We live in a fast-paced, high pressured, loud society. When we vacation, we try to slow down, unwind from our pressures, and minimize the media impact around us. Whether this is done in a lawn chair in the backyard, or on an island with coconut and palm trees, we all need to catch up, rest up, and regroup our priorities. A special needs student has difficulty with doing this on even a minimal level. Stresses are magnified and controlling dynamics is next to impossible without assistance. Organically, these students may lack certain balance in their brain functions which cause them to need assistance in training themselves to balance their thinking minds and their feeling or emotional minds in their one brain. Dr. William Glasser, a practicing psychiatrist psychotherapist and educator, says that behavior is "knowledge in action."

The Nassau County Board of Cooperative Educational Services gave Glasser training to all staff in the special educational division. The purpose of this instructional training was to help all students in the program manage their behavior more responsibly. Based on the three-point program described in *Stations of the Mind* (William Glasser, Harper & Row, 1982), teachers were trained to help their students: (1) understand behavior, both theirs and others; (2) learn and use responsible and effective behavior to make a good and successful life in school; (3) develop social skills that would produce a responsible and successful life in the community. His theory is called Choice Theory, developed from the Control Theory of William Powers. Dr. Glasser helps teachers organize their schools 'into environments that create a better quality of living—ideals of a good life start in the music, math, art, dance, language arts, social studies, science, athletic programs, etc., where a student's physical and psychological needs are interwoven in their daily activities. Four basic needs should be addressed properly in each discipline.

1. Belonging. Students need to be connected to their world. They need to be with people who know and care about them and to know that they are accepted and appreciated. (This is quite hard, for example, when the student in your music class has just been notified by social services that his foster parent is not going to adopt him but is going to adopt his baby sister. How can you expect him to play softly on the drumset?)
2. Gaining power. A student will grow in knowledge and skill and gain self-esteem through success. Dr. Glasser feels that competence is its foundation, accomplishment its developer, and confidence its empowering expression. Through modeling a musical activity, the student will gain power by his successful mastery of same through realistic teacher direction.
3. Having fun. Having fun improves health, builds positive relationships, and enhances thinking. No matter how diverse the students are in the music classroom, activities need to have laughter. The students need to be uplifted and spirited to add to the quality of their successful program.
4. Being free. All students—disturbed, challenged, or gifted (mainstreamed or not)—need to express control of their own lives, They need to set goals, make plans, choose behaviors, evaluate results, and learn from each experience to do things better.

When a student is responsible for making his own good life when things go right, he can feel satisfied and secure. When things go wrong, the student is distressed and needs help to set things right. There are countless examples in newspapers, magazines, radio, television, and the cinema about the benefits of music study. To illustrate the good life concept of Glasser, I would like to recall the movie character Gertrude Lang in *Mr. Holland's Opus*. The Honorable Governor Gertrude Lang was ready to give up playing the clarinet in the high school band that Mr. Holland conducted.

Try as she might, she felt that she was holding the other players back by her lack of good technique and tone. Mr. Holland would not let her give up. Instead, he realized he needed to apply another teaching strategy for Ms. Lang. Mr. Holland asked Ms. Lang whether playing the clarinet was any fun. He said that music is "about heart, about feelings, about moving people, something beautiful, and being alive. ... It's not about notes on a page."

Then Mr. Holland asked Ms. Lang something personal: what she liked about herself when she looked in the mirror. She replied her hair because her father said it reminded him of the sunset. Mr. Holland then asked Ms. Lang to close her eyes and play the sunset on the clarinet. Ms. Lang let her imagination bring out the music in her soul, and it worked!

What do we learn from this? To some it is obvious. To others it is not. Help is needed to supply beautiful images of a sunset, sunrise, colors in the rainbow, swans on a lake. Through music and the sounds of nature we can assist in building up the shattered lives of our special students. Besides the wonderful sounds of nature on recordings, cassettes, or compact discs, digital keyboards with their extraordinary sound banks can often help students experience both hearing the common and the exotic and beautiful. After students have a foundation of the natural harmonic sounds of nature, we can open the doors for active listening experiences with the great music literature.

In summary, music educators can profoundly affect the mental health and welfare of their students by teaching about peace, harmony, beauty, calm, silence, love, and laughter. If the environment in the music classroom has the four basic elements of the good life—belonging, gaining power, having fun, and being free, then by teaching about the soft sounds of life our students can begin to develop a broad range of dynamics. This repertoire will serve as a key to their success for a better quality of student's inner life. As music educators, we can help our highly charged, emotionally disturbed students manage their moods using crescendo and loud for emphasis and decrescendo and soft to show gentleness, kindness, and sensitivity. The late Pablo Casals, renowned cellist, humanitarian, and conductor, taught of life through his words and music: "We are one of the leaves of a tree, and the tree is all humanity. A musician, as every man, must take part in the movement of the world."

With these tools our students can separate

their aggression from the task at hand and show control of their hands and hearts at the drumset, on the tambourines, and with maracas. Their own storms which rage within can become more self-manageable. With a repertoire of the peaceful sounds of nature, music becomes colorful, not monotone. Through the range of sounds, students will soon be able to successfully play not only loud, louder, loudest, but soft, softer, softest.

This article first appeared in the December 1998 issue of New York's The School Music News. *Reprinted by permission.*

Instrumental Music Education and the Academic Achievement of Special Learners

Candace T. Still

Much attention has been given to the impact of musical training on brain development and academic achievement in recent years. While some claims have been perhaps overstated, particularly in the popular media, the amount of reliable literature is growing. Many studies have been replicated without contradiction, which validates their findings and contributions to the literature from the medical and scientific communities.

Best known is the research conducted at the University of California at Irvine on the brain development and academic achievement of music students. The impetus for these studies came from the hypothesis of Gordon Shaw and Xiaodan Leng that there exists "a causal connection between music training and spatial ability." Basically, they proposed that the mental processing of musical information builds "neural firing patterns" in localized sections of the brain that are interconnected over large portions of the cerebral cortex. Shaw and Leng joined forces with Frances Rauscher to investigate further. After a small pilot study in 1993, the team conducted a study of the relationship between music and the brain's ability to reason in other areas. Preschool students in a middle-income school and an at-risk school listened to a Mozart sonata and then were administered a test for spatial IQ. Spatial reasoning was also measured after sessions of listening to relaxation instructions and silence. The results yielded what is now known as the "Mozart effect," a temporary increase in spatial IQ. No such effect was noted after subjects experienced 10 minutes of silence or 10 minutes of relaxation instructions. This study was replicated twice, yielding the same results (Rauscher, 1996). While these findings have been exaggerated and, at times, overstated, they have been the springboards for subsequent studies in the areas of music cognition.

In 1994 Rauscher's team conducted a study of the effect of keyboard lessons on spatial reasoning. Kindergarten students who received eight months of keyboard lessons demonstrated a 46 percent increase in spatial IQ over their peers who received no keyboard lessons. A similar study was conducted in 1997 to eliminate the influence of the Hawthorne effect, the possibility that any new stimulus or experience will temporarily yield positive results just because it is new. In this study the control groups received computer lessons, casual singing experiences, or no enrichment experience at all. The group that received piano lessons scored significantly higher than all of the control groups in spatial-temporal reasoning (Rauscher, 1999).

Probably the most significant data produced by Rauscher's team placed this type of musical training in a public school classroom setting. After eight months, kindergarten students who received class keyboard lessons exhibited a 48 percent greater increase in spatial-temporal skills than did their peers who received no music lessons (Rauscher, 1999).

In addition to the Rauscher research, other studies have been conducted in the last decade to investigate the theory that students who receive musical training exhibit greater cognitive function. For example, students in two Rhode Island elementary schools received a sequential, skill-building music enrichment program (the "test art" program) while students in a control group did not. Before receiving the enrichment, the percentage of "test art" students at or above the national average in scores on the kindergarten Metropolitan Achievement Tests (MAT) was far behind that of the control group. After seven months, all students took the first-grade MAT. Test results revealed that only 55 percent of the control group students were at grade level or above in mathematics, in comparison with 77 percent of the "test art" students. The two groups were equal in reading scores. The project was continued for a second year, with tests yielding the same results (Gardner et al., 1996).

While the number of studies on the relationship between musical training and cognitive function grows and is validated, only a small portion of the literature addresses the possibility that special needs learners might enjoy the same benefits as regular students. The concept of teaching instrumental music to special needs students is relatively new, and the sparse literature that exists deals primarily with adaptations and/or incorporation of special education strategies in the music classroom (Zdzinski, 2001).

It is interesting to note that Howard Gardner's earlier research was done on brain-damaged adults. His study of linguistic processing by the human brain revealed that language and music stimulate the same areas of the brain. The complexity of this relationship is evident in aphasic musicians, those who have lost the ability to use or understand language. Gardner's studies further revealed that, while most people learn basic musical skills in the same way, the manner in which that information is organized in the brain may differ dramatically from person to person. The effect of brain damage on musicians is often more complex than on other artists because of the complex mental roles a musician plays in processing music and the variety of skills that are used in combination at any given moment (Gardner, 1982).

Of importance is the fact that Gardner recognized a correlation between brain organization in brain-damaged adults and learning-disabled children. For example, adults with reading disorders (alexias) exhibited processing abilities and patterns similar to those of children with dyslexia, and specific calculation disorders in adults were akin to specific problems learning disabled children may have had with learning arithmetic. The conclusion Gardner drew is that children may actually be born with neurological impairments that resemble processing patterns found in adults with brain injuries.

It seems reasonable, therefore, that if a brain-damaged adult can regain lost function, even in part, through rehabilitation, a learning-disabled child might, through some rehabilitative measure, be able to develop cognitive functions otherwise impossible. Furthermore, if normal children who learn to play a musical instrument can demonstrate greater cognitive ability and brain function, teaching learning-disabled children to play an instrument could possibly contribute to the creation of bilateral networks for overcoming the obstacles these students face. Chadwick and Clark (1980) recognized music as a motivator in working with physically handicapped students because bilateral processing in music in the brain enabled physically disabled people to respond to music, regardless of their level of function.

Eric Jensen, in *Brain-Based Learning and Teaching* (1995), maintains that processing music affects both hemispheres of the brain, and that the entire body responds to music through muscle energy, metabolism, and emotion. He, as well as Gardner, have discovered the cognitive connection between linguistic skills and musical skills. Could an instrumental music education be an intervention for children with certain learning disabilities?

Purpose

The purpose of this study was to compare the standardized reading test scores of middle school instrumental music students (those enrolled in band or orchestra) who receive special education services with other special education students who are not enrolled in the instrumental music program.

Methodology

Research Design. This study employed a two-group comparison design. To identify the two groups, students who were enrolled in an instrumental music program, either band or orchestra, will be referred to as the "Music" group, and students who were not enrolled in an instrumental music program will be referred to as the "Non-Music" group. For the purpose of this study, standardized reading test scores of 175 special education students were compiled. Seventy-two students reported inconclusive scores due to transience, absenteeism, or failure to complete both pre- and posttests. Elimination of those scores yielded a pool of 103 sets of scores for comparison.

The study pool was disaggregated according to disability classification. Initial survey of scores for students classified as "other health impaired" (OHI) revealed a degree of inconsistency in individual scores that precluded them from this study. OHI in this case indicated students with attention deficit disorder (ADD) or attention deficit with hyperactivity disorder (ADHD). Possible explanations of such inconsistencies included varied testing times throughout the school day, student use of medication for attention management, and lack of comprehension of testing mechanics on the part of the student. The final pool included 68 sets of scores for comparison from 58 learning disabled (LD) and 10 emotionally/ behavior-disordered (EBD) students. Further examination of scores among LD and EBD students were broken down into Music and Non-Music groups, creating four test subgroups: LD Music, LD Non-Music, BD Music, and BD Nonmusic. All of the scores generated by the testing instrument were evaluated for each of the four separate subgroups.

Instrument. The data collected were student scores from the Standardized Test of Assessment of Reading (STAR™) (Advantage Learning Systems, 1997). STAR is a norm-referenced and criterion-referenced reading test that provides estimates of student reacting scores (relative to national norms) to teachers, students, and parents on an ongoing basis throughout the school year, providing reliable data on reading growth. Four norm-referenced scores have been used in this study to provide a relative comparison of individual student reading achievement to the group of students who took the test at the same time. One criterion-referenced score was also considered to provide feedback on how student growth should be interpreted in comparison to the national standard for STAR.

STAR reports five different types of test scores. Scores include the Scaled Score, the Grade Equivalent, the Instructional Reading Level, Percentile Rank, and the Normal Curve Equivalent. All of the information on these test scores has been derived from the *Star Norms/Technical Manual*, which accompanies the software.

- The Scaled Score (SS) is a norm-referenced score that is derived by comparing students' test scores and converting them to a common scale. A proprietary Bayesian statistical model is used by STAR to derive the SS, which ranges from 50 to 1350.
- The Grade Equivalent (GE) is assigned according to student performance in comparison to the median score of students in each grade. For example, if the median score of all fifth-grade students in their sixth month were 440, then anyone who scored 440 would be assigned a GE of 5.6. GE is a norm-referenced score.
- Similar to GE is the Instructional Reading Level (IRL), which is a criterion-referenced score. The IRL estimates the most appropriate reading level for students tested based on word recognition and comprehension of test material. In the field of reading assessment, IRL is defined as "the highest reading level at which the student can answer 80 percent or more of the items correctly" (STAR, 1997).
- Percentile Rank (PR) is another snapshot of how an individual performed on this particular test on one particular day, in comparison with his or her national peers. For example, a student has a PR of 90 performed at a level higher than 90 percent of students in the same grade at the national level. STAR PRs range from 1to 99. It is a norm-referenced score.
- Normal Curve Equivalent (NCE) is a norm-referenced score that refers to the conversion of the PR to an equal-measure scale for use in comparing STAR scores to other achievement tests. NCE scores are also used for computing averages and interpolating test scores.

Data Collection. Students were given the STAR pretest on networked computers in the language arts classrooms during the language arts class period, making it necessary to spread out the pretest period over a period of eight weeks. STAR generated a pretest score for each student in each of the five categories described above. The posttest was given in the same manner. Posttest scores were recorded for each student in each of the five categories.

Analysis. Pre- and posttest scores were compared to evaluate the amount of growth each student experienced in each of the five scoring categories. For each of the test groups, the Music group and the Non-Music group, the mean score was determined in each category for both the pre- and posttests. The pretest mean score was subtracted from the posttest mean to calculate the growth mean score in each category for each of the test groups. Growth means were analyzed in comparing the Music group to the Non-Music group to determine if there was an appreciable difference between the two.

Findings

In every scoring category, in each disability classification, the Music group exhibited higher mean growth scores than did the Non-Music group. Likewise, in each of the four subgroups, the Music group outperformed the Non-Music group in every category. The GE growth mean for the LD Music subgroup was .7, or 7 months, while the GE growth mean for the LD Non-Music subgroup was .1, a performance difference of 6 months. The BD Music subgroups showed a net growth in GE of 2 years and 3 months (2.3), while the BD Non-Music subgroup only posted a net gain of 2 months yielding a performance difference of 2.1 or 2 years and 1 month (Figure 1).

Similar trends hold true for all other scoring categories. Figure 2 illustrates the SS. LD Music students had a net growth mean score of 80, but their Non-Music counterparts only netted a growth mean of 7. The BD Music subgroup gained an impressive 271 points in SS. The BD Non- Music students, however, only gained 31 points in their SS growth mean.

The trend in the PR and NCE indicated even more serious growth problems in the Non-Music subgroups. Both the LD and BD Music subgroups posted positive mean growth scores in these categories. Figure 3 represents change in Percentile Rank of students in the study in comparison with their national peers. The LD Music students showed a growth mean of 3 percentile in PR and 1.9 in NCE. The BD Music students netted a PR gain of 18 percentile and an NCE gain of 13.7 points.

Figure 4 represents the NCE's of students in the study, which relate to the national PR as a converted score.

In contrast, the LD Non-Music students lost 5 percentile points and 1.9 NCE points and the BD Non-Music students lost 7 and 4.8 points respectively. The negative growth in the Non-Music subgroups is an indication that these students have fallen farther behind, while their Music counterparts have shown healthy growth.

The only criterion-referenced score in STAR shows a continuation of the same trend between the Music and Non-Music subgroups. IRL scores of LD Music students indicate a gain of 6 months in IRL over the LD Non-Music subgroup. More significantly, the BD Music students increased their mean IRL 2.1 years over Non-Music students (Figure 5).

Conclusions

Special education students in every disability group, subgroup, and scoring category who were enrolled in a band or orchestra program exhibited higher mean growth scores calculated from STAR (Table 1). Furthermore, students with emotional/ behavior disorders showed even more growth over their Non-Music counterparts than did the learning-disabled music students, indicating that another dimension may exist to the cognitive benefit instrumental music instruction provides EBD students.

Discussion

While this study indicates that the reading growth of the instrumental music students was superior, it is prudent to make note of several factors that may or may not have affected the results. The number of score from EBD students is fairly low, consisting of only five Music students and five Non-Music students. More convincing evidence might be obtained through replication of the study using a larger group of EBD students. It is also important to note that students whose scores were entered into the project did not take STAR pretests and postttests at the same time, or even on the same day. This factor alone may have some bearing on the inconsistency of OHI scores, which were ultimately precluded from the study. In addition, some students scored very high, while others scored far below grade level. As students reach the top end of the forming scale, greater academic gain is required to improve their scores. Conversely, it takes less academic gain to raise the scores of a deficient reader in comparison to the norm.

Also, these findings might be further substantiated by replicating this study on a districtwide or statewide scale. Further credence might also be accrued by measuring reading achievement via other nationally recognized standardized tests over a period of several years and by measuring the reading achievement of students who receive services in other areas of special education. Concurring results could have substantial implications for the use of instrumental music instruction as a cognitive intervention for special education students.

References

Chadwick, D. M., & Clark, C. A. (1980). Adapting music instruments for the physically handicapped. *Music Educators Journal* 67(3), 56–59

Gardner, H. (1982). *Art mind and brain: A cognitive approach to creativity*. Boston: Basic Books.

Gardner. M., Fox, A., Knowles, F., & Jeffrey, D. (1996). Learning improved by arts training [Online]. *Nature*. May 23, 1996 issue.

Jensen, E. (1995). *Brain-based learning and teaching*. Del Mar, CA: Turning Point.

Rauscher, F. H. (1996). Music exposure and the development of spatial intelligence in children. *Bulletin of the Council for Research in Music Education*, 142, 35–47.

Rauscher, F. H. (1999). What educators must learn from science: The case for music in the schools. *Voice: The Washington Music Education Association Journal*. Available: http://www.menc.org/publication/articles/academic/academic.htm.

Zdzinski, S. F. (2001). Instrumental music for special learners. *Music Educators Journal*, 87 (4), 27–35.

This article first appeared in the Summer 2003 issue of the Georgia Music News. *Reprinted by permission.*

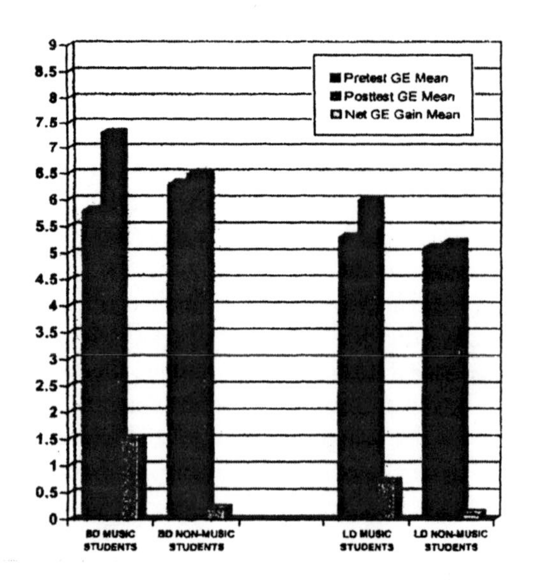

Figure 1. Grade equivalent mean growth for BD and LD students

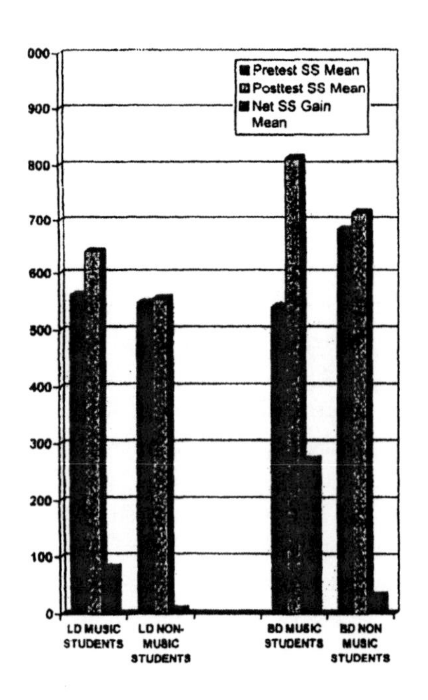

Figure 2. Standard-score growth mean for LD and BD students

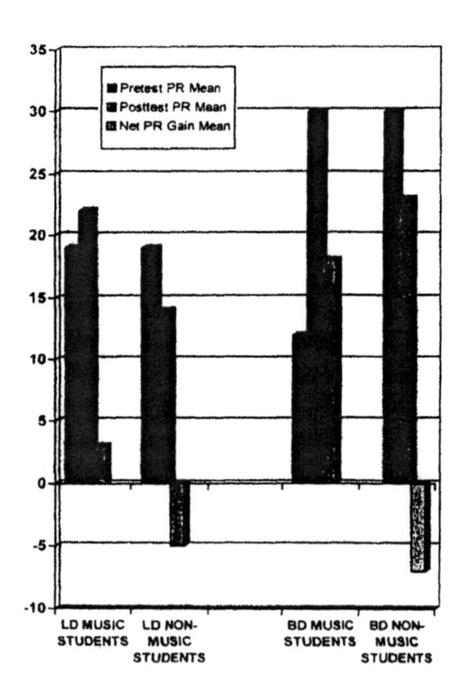

Figure 3. Percentile rank of LD and BD students

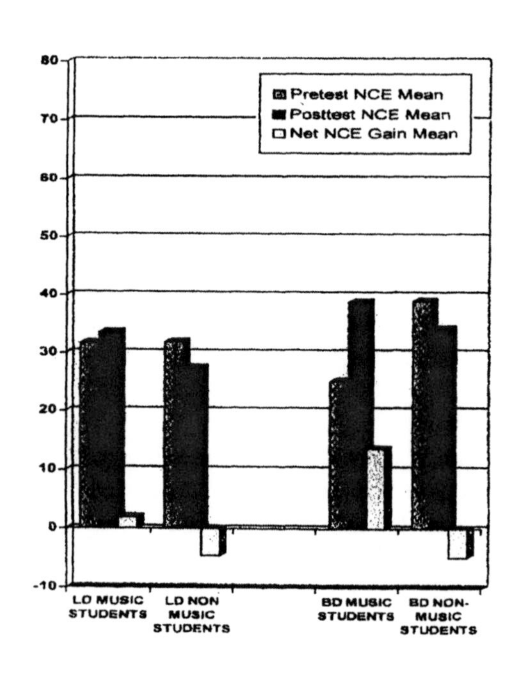

Figure 4. Normal-curve equivalent for LD and BD students

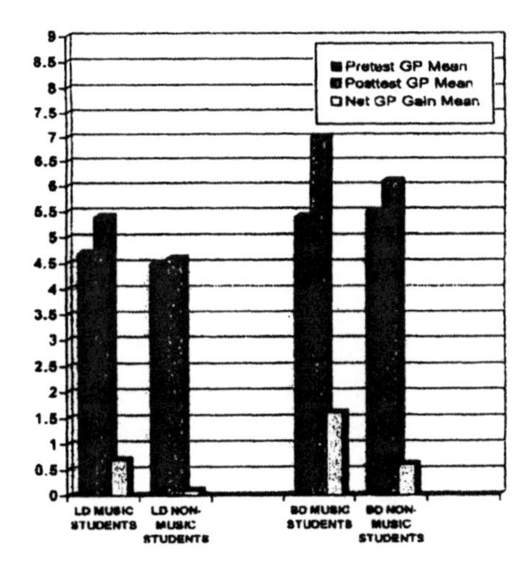

Figure 5. Instructional reading level for LD and BD students

	GE	*SS*	*PR*	*NCE*	*IRL*
LD Music Pretest	5.3	561	19	31.7	4.7
LD Music Posttest	6.0	641	22	33.6	5.4
LD Non-Music Pretest	5.1	548	19	31.9	4.5
LD Non-Music Posttest	5.2	555	14	27.4	4.6
BD Music Pretest	5.8	624	30	38.8	5.4
BD Music Posttest	7.3	806	43	46.2	7.0
BD Non-Music Pretest	6.3	683	30	39.0	5.5
BD Non-Music Posttest	6.5	714	23	34.2	6.1

Table 1. Overview of STAR scores measured in this study

On Teaching and Interacting with Blind Students

Ryan Strunk

Since my birth almost twenty-one years ago, I have been blind. I have not been visually impaired, nor visually challenged, nor hard of seeing. I was born blind, and this suits me well.

Long before my birth almost twenty-one years ago, researchers, scientists, and the like have sought to understand the blind. They have devised programs aimed at aiding the blind, but too often, they develop their methods and carry out their research either without consulting the supposed beneficiaries of their services, or by drawing broad generalizations which do little more than confuse issues. They draw conclusions based on their beliefs alone, and this I find hard to stomach.

Of course, this is not always the case. Sometimes, researchers have sought input from the blind, and as might be expected, the programs and tools they have developed have performed above and beyond their expectations. In my career as a musician and in my studies as a choral music education major, I have actively encouraged this communication between myself and my colleagues and professors; often, I have received it.

In recent research, however, I have unearthed articles and documents which would suggest that not all are as open-minded as my professors and fellow students—articles which divulge broad, general, and often misleading statements about the blind. The materials I have found, though almost certainly printed with the sincerest of intentions, possess the ability to lead readers to false conclusions, based on the false information they provide. For example: In many early residential schools for the blind, students were instructed in the art of tuning pianos. This was done because it was generally believed that blind people, in addition to their extremely high degree of musical ability, usually possessed perfect pitch. Had the planners of these schools ever met some of the blind people I know, they might quickly have changed their ... tune.

In an article which appeared in the February 2002 issue of the *American String Teachers Association Journal* entitled "Rewards and Challenges of Teaching Blind String Students," author Stacey Hessler-Binder draws an interesting conclusion about said pupils. Blind students, Hessler-Binder believes, respond particularly well to imagery involving food. When she desires a legato sound from them, she tells them to play like rich chocolate fudge. When she desires a crisp sound, she tells her blind students "to think of the freshest salad ever."

I find Ms. Hessler-Binder's advice to be quite good in a certain respect. Imagery, we often learn, can prove instrumental in reaching a desired goal. Crisp apples, fresh salads, thick hot fudge, and gooey molasses will certainly provide quality imagery for almost every student in the classroom. Thus, is it necessary for the author to draw the conclusion that it is the blind who respond particularly well to food? I would submit, rather, that everyone can relate to vittles, be they blind or sighted.

I have had dealings in past years with a particular educator who seems to be of a mind that because of my blindness, my other senses must certainly be heightened. He often tells me something to the effect of "Ryan, you hear things with your marvelous ears that none of us can even comprehend." In addition to being false, this teacher's assertion, though placing a positive light on me, serves to set me apart from my fellow musicians.

Neither of the above assertions, I am certain, were meant to be harmful in any respect. However, both of them lack the essential element that we the blind desire most—equality with our sighted counterparts. They seem to say "yes, the blind are worthy and capable, but they are still different."

As a blind college student working toward a job in the public school system, I certainly do not wish for this distinction to be so prevalent. Because of this, I do the same work as that required of my fellow students, and I make no exceptions to remove responsibility from my shoulders. I have always believed that blind people are just as capable as the sighted, and I and others have striven to make this notion a reality to those around us. With the same opportunities as those afforded to the sighted, and a touch of creativity, the music experience for blind students can be just as rewarding and challenging as it is for the sighted.

Reference

Hessler-Binder, Stacey. Rewards and challenges of teaching blind string students. *American String Teachers Journal*, February 2002, 80–85.

This article first appeared in the April 2004 issue of the Nebraska Music Educator. *Reprinted by permission.*

A Little Help from Your (Music Therapy) Friends

Rebecca Tweedle

In the "Special Learners" column of the February-March issue, you read about a study conducted by Darrow (1999) in which music educators' main concern about inclusive education was cited as the need for collaboration with other professionals who are knowledgeable about students with disabilities. This may very well be a concern of yours also. If so, you may be asking, "Where can I find professionals who have a comprehensive understanding of both music and disabilities and who can give me specific suggestions for adapting lesson plans, understanding goals on my students' Individual Education Plan (IEP), and managing behavior?" The answer may lie in music therapy.

Music therapy can be defined as the therapeutic use of music to address physical, psychological, cognitive, and social functioning. As a profession, music therapy became widely recognized during World War II, with training programs beginning in Michigan and Kansas in the 1950s. Individuals wishing to become music therapists take courses in the fundamentals of music (theory, history, etc.), behavioral and health sciences (psychology, anatomy, etc.), and music therapy (influence of music on behavior, functional music therapy skills, etc.). Following coursework, students complete a six-month internship that results in eligibility to sit for the national certification exam. Upon passing the exam, the individual is granted the credential Music Therapist—Board Certified (MTBC). (Professional designations of RMT and CMT may also used to identify those who are qualified to provide music therapy clinical services.) Today, the American Music Therapy Association (AMTA) represents over 4,000 music therapists around the country. In Ohio alone, there are currently more than 150 music therapists practicing in a variety of settings including hospitals, day treatment centers, early intervention centers, nursing homes, and schools.

Music therapy and music education are similar in many ways. Both fields require a bachelor's degree for entry-level practice; both require a major instrument or vocal emphasis and course work in music theory, history, and conducting; and both require fieldwork. Most important, the emphasis in both professions is on helping others achieve their potential through music.

Differences between the professions do exist, however. Music educators take music methods courses while music therapists take courses that prepare them to use music therapeutically. Information about various disabilities is included in the music therapy coursework. The fieldwork for a music educator is performed in an education setting, while the fieldwork for a music therapist must be performed in a variety of settings, some of which may be educational. The main difference between the two fields, however, is in the role of music: In music education the musical product is the fundamental goal, while in music therapy music is the means through which goals (largely nonmusical) are accomplished. Such goals relate to the areas of academic, motor, communicative, and social/emotional functioning.

In a school setting, music therapy may be recognized as a related service similar to speech, occupational, or physical therapy. Frequently, the music therapist is a member of an interdisciplinary team consisting of the special education teacher, psychologist, classroom teacher, and the above-mentioned related services. Music therapy can address many of the IEP goals that are developed by this interdisciplinary team. Preacademic and academic skills, such as learning numbers, colors, or reading and writing can be learned or enhanced through music activities. Motor skills can be addressed through a variety of movement activities, including individual movement, group movement, and movement with props such as beanbags and parachutes. Communication abilities are increased through chanting, singing, and using augmentative communication devices. Social and emotional skills are fostered in group activities where students learn to participate as a group member, share instruments, and wait for their turn.

There are three fundamental roles that a music therapist can play in a school setting to assist music educators. The first is that of a consultant. In this role, the therapist suggests ways to adapt instruments, modify lesson plans, or modify challenging behaviors. The second role is that of a direct service provider. In this role, the music therapist attends the regular music class with the special needs child in order to assist him or her in developing the skills needed to succeed in the class. As a direct service provider, the therapist conducts music sessions for a self-contained classroom of students with special needs. Sometimes, the therapist works with children on an individual basis in order to help them acquire skills necessary to succeed in the classroom. The third role is that of an in-service provider. In this role, the therapist provides training for the music educators in a school district or individual facility. Training topics include understanding the language of special education, the categories and characteristics of special needs, adaptive devices and interventions, and behavior management strategies.

There are a variety of publications that may assist music educators who work with students with special needs. The list included here is not meant to be all-inclusive; rather, it may offer a starting point for further investigation.

Music educators and music therapists share the aim of providing all students with opportunities to experience success in music. Hopefully, the information in this article will stimulate collaboration as we strive to attain this worthy goal.

Publications

Birkenshaw-Fleming, L. (1993). *Music for all.* Toronto, Canada: Gordon V. Thompson Music.

Clark, C. & Chadwick, D. (1980). *Clinically adapted instruments for the multiply handicapped.* St. Louis, MO: MMB Music, Inc.

Darrow, A. A. (1999). Music educators' perceptions regarding the inclusion of students with severe disabilities in music classrooms. *Journal of Music Therapy*, 36(4), 254–273.

Hughes, J. & Robbins, B. *Mainstreaming in School Music K–12* . Leon County Schools. 904-487-7160.

Humpal, M. & Dimmick, J. (March, 1995). Special learners in the music classroom. *Music Educators Journal.*

Journal of Music Therapy. Published quarterly by the American Music Therapy Association.

Music Therapy Perspectives. Published by the American Music Therapy Association.

Schaberg, G. (Ed.). (1988). *Tips: Teaching Music to Special Learners.* Reston, VA: MENC.

Wilson, B. (Ed.). (1996). *Models of music therapy intervention in school settings: From institution to inclusion.* Silver Spring, MD: American Music Therapy Association.

This article first appeared in the May–June 2000 issue of Ohio's TRIAD. *Reprinted by permission.*

Standards and the Special Learner

Judie Wass

With the introduction of standards for music education, there are concerns being expressed regarding the needs of special-education students. Some of this concern is understandable; however, with increased knowledge of some adaptations, accommodations, and modifications possible, you can see these students become successful learners.

Adaptations are changes made to the environment, curriculum instruction, and/ or assessment practices in order for a student to be a successful learner. Adaptations include: (1) accommodation and (2) modifications.

Adaptations:

- are based on individual students' strengths and needs.
- may vary in intensity and degree.

Accommodations are provisions made in *how* a student accesses and demonstrates learning. These do not substantially change the instructional level, the content, or the performance criteria. The changes are made in order to provide a student equal access to learning and equal opportunity to demonstrate what is known.

Accommodations include changes in and/or provision of the following:

- presentation and/or response format and procedures
- instructional strategies
- time/scheduling
- attitudes
- architecture
- environment
- equipment

Modifications are substantial changes in *what* a student is expected to learn and demonstrate. These changes are made to provide a student opportunities to participate meaningfully and productively in learning experiences and environments.

Modifications include changes in the following:

- instructional level
- content
- performance criteria

Note that under Colorado Section 4, 2253-401 et sequ. C.R.S., a student must have a special-education Individualized Education Plan (IEP) to qualify for modifications to the standards. These modifications should be written into the IEP.

It is important to consider the following basic assumptions when using adaptations:

- It is necessary to clearly state what all students are to know and be able to do before determining whether a specific adaptation is an accommodation or modification.
- It is important to consider adaptations for both instruction and assessment. When students need adaptations in how they learn, they will usually need adaptations in how they are assessed.
- Accommodations and modifications must be determined for each student based on his or her individual strengths and needs, and on his or her immediate context. Students who require accommodations in some areas may need modifications in other areas.
- The more intense a student's needs, the more likely it is that he or she will need adaptations. Students who require modifications will probably also require accommodation.

Below, I have gathered some ideas that I use in my own classroom that can be labeled as adaptations, accommodation, or modifications. I have found these to be useful in making the special student a successful learner. My hope is that these will be of some assistance to you and not require a great deal of your valuable time.

- Pairing the special child with another student has been very successful in integrated classrooms. It alleviates some of the demands on me and is of benefit to both students. It has developed some very positive relationships within classrooms.
- Making minor modifications to Orff instruments and rhythm instruments gives the students more opportunities to participate. Adding foam to the handle of a mallet for the student who needs help with gripping would be an example. (This is related to Colorado Standard No. 1.)
- When using textbooks or written materials, use highlighting and colored pencils for key elements of the lesson. This can assist the student in focusing on the important aspects of the lesson.
- I often send tapes or CDs of materials covered in music to homeroom teachers. This technique gives the students more exposure to the lesson covered. They listen on headphones during free time and breaks. (This is related to Standard No. 4.)
- I am now preparing "music bags" for checkout by special learners. The students take them home with them for two to three days and then return them to me. Some of the items included in the bags are: (1) tapes of *Peter and the Wolf*, *Carnival of the Animals* and other classics, along with suggested activities such as art to music (this is related to Standard No. 4); (2)

a recorder, a small keyboard, or other instrument with picture and stick notation (this is related to Standards Nos. 1 and 2); (3) a sing-along tape and book (this is related to Standard No. 1); (4) music games such as notation dominoes and pencil puzzles (this is related to Standard No. 2); and (5) picture books and stories about music (this could address several standards depending on the book).

- *Opportunities for Success* is a book that has been distributed to each school in the state by the State Department of Education. The purpose of this book is to provide assistance to all teachers who work with special-education students. It has a wealth of information to assist you. This book should be available through your special-education department or resource teacher.

I wish you much success and great rewards working with special learners.

This article first appeared in the Summer 1997 issue of the Colorado Music Educator. *Reprinted by permission.*

Teaching Those Challenging Students and Making It a Success!

Linda Weyman

Teaching at Sacred Hearts Academy for the past three years has been my first teaching experience in a private school. Because of my many other years (I won't say how many) in public schools, I know that there is concern and stress regarding the "mainstreaming" or "inclusion" of some students. I would like to share some of my experiences and observations through the years.

During my years in Pittsburgh, I was fortunate to be chosen to participate in a three-year U. S. Department of Education grant on the Inclusion of Special Needs students into the regular classroom. Included in this grant project were classroom teachers, special education teachers, specialists, administrators, principals, and counselors. The research aspect of the grant was conducted as an "action research" project with the assistance of a team from the Allegheny-Singer Research Institute who came into the classroom to act as a "third eye" or a "critical friend." These three years were a priceless opportunity for me to expand my understanding and skills.

My other experience, the one that has changed my life the most, is that of a parent of a special needs child. (Special needs was the term used when we went through the public school system together.) Unless you have experienced the daily battles and struggles that you encounter as a parent and child, you have no idea what it's like. Both of us still wear battle scars and deal with them daily.

Thus, how do we make these experiences a success for all students? When we are teaching students who may have a learning disability such as Attention Deficit Hyperactivity Disorder (ADHD) or an emotional problem along with 25 or more other individuals, how do we make it work? A music educator recently said to me, "We have to treat them just like any other student." My first reaction to this comment was a resounding "No!" First of all, each student comes to us with his or her own background, strengths and weaknesses, and expectations. We don't treat any individual like all of the rest. We need to remember that we don't teach music, we teach people.

My second instinct is to say, "Read the IEP!" The IEP (Indiviudalized Education Plan) is a legal, binding document between the school, the student, and the parents. Don't jeopardize your teaching career by ignoring this important contract. Study it so that you know what you are dealing with: the strengths and weaknesses.

Let's talk a little bit about those strengths and weaknesses. What I have found in my own teaching is that these "special students" are often very gifted in something. That something is often found in the arts. Not only are they often gifted and musically talented, but they find a productive outlet for pent-up emotion, energy, and anger through music. The problem some of us run into when teaching these students is that we are still looking at our subject areas in the academic mode. Even if we are still stuck on that concept, we must bend our style to correlate with the student's IEP. Therefore, do not ask a student who is dyslexic to take a timed test and expect success. What you see as frustration and failure will turn into behavior problems. Your classroom management will sail out the door and you will be calling the parents so that they can hear for the hundredth time how awful their child is in class. What do you do? First, try to find their strengths. Let me give you an example:

Larry was an extremely hyperactive third grader. He was the kind of boy who would come into the classroom, sit down, and fall off his chair. He was the one who gave ADHD its name. Well, I noticed that Larry really liked to whistle, and he whistled well. (Often he whistled when I didn't want him to whistle.) "Let's make this negative into a positive," I thought. Larry had a very bad self-image. I decided that Larry needed a positive experience in his life. I told him that I thought he was an excellent whistler, and asked him if he would do a very special part for our program—a whistling part! The deal was that he could only whistle when he was asked to, and not disrupt at other times. It worked, and he was the best whistler on the song, "It Ain't Gonna Rain No More." The faculty and students were astounded at Larry's gift, and he was proud of himself, maybe for the first time in his life. Better yet, his parents were seeing their son in a positive light for the first time in a very long time.

So, whenever you are at your wit's end with a student with challenges, think of Larry. Think of what it would be like to have high intelligence and not be able to read or to have so much energy that you feel like jumping out of your skin. Understand where some of the anger and emotional outbursts come from and do something. Be a teacher!

This article first appeared in the April 2000 issue of Hawaii's HMEA Bulletin. *Reprinted by permission.*

Other MENC Special Learners Resources

TIPS: Teaching Music to Special Learners.
Compiled by Gail Schaberg. 1988. 40 pages. #1092.

For complete ordering information on these and other publications, contact:

MENC
Publications Sales
1806 Robert Fulton Drive
Reston, VA 20191-4348

Credit card holders may call 1-800-828-0229

Breinigsville, PA USA
26 May 2010
238783BV00001B/18/P

9 781565 451674